LITANY
OF LOONS

LITANY
OF LOONS

Jack Truett

To order additional copies of this book, contact:
Xlibris Corporation
1-888-795-4274
www.Xlibris.com
Orders@Xlibris.com

FOREWORD

Shortly before D-Day of World War Two, I stood in a very old dungeon looking at some of the original torture machines that had been used for countless, hideous butcherings of humans during the hundreds of years of the Inquisition. For many years this horrible period of human blundering and cruelty has been taught to the Catholic Priesthood as the "Spanish" Inquisition. Such a determined and thorough job of this has been done, that today almost all of our Christian herds know no other information about the insane carnage, for the truth of the matter has been thoroughly purged, altered, or deleted from most school texts and public libraries. One has to now dig very diligently and deeply to find any real truth about the thing left anywhere.

Spain during those centuries was one of the most powerful and "Christian" Nations in the world. More Cathedrals and Catholic Priests were present in its borders than any other country, even more so than in the Vatican's own territory. Thus they *were* one of the main leaders in ALL Catholic endeavors, including Inquisition horrors. But they were *not*, as today's clergy believes and teaches, a "splinter" cult that had been excommunicated by the Vatican. They were in fact diligently following the edicts of the Vatican and its "infallible" Popes who instigated and directed centuries of atrocities now quaintly known as the "Spanish Inquisition." Any in depth true summary of these centuries and their horrors would fill a fairly large library. I was doing my best to be a Christian, which created in me a very real need to look for the truth, particularly since the war left me with no great ability to do otherwise.

But the war ended and I had to forget a lot of things and try to earn a living. My wife and I suddenly found ourselves with two young daughters. Then in quick succession, four sons and another daughter were born to us. I couldn't even afford a job any longer, let alone the countless non-earning hours required for writing a book. My only tool for writing was a decrepit old Royal with faded ribbon and poorly aligned, smudged keys, sad production machinery indeed to create manuscripts for futzie editors. So the old typewriter lay moldering, my research for material went on hold, and my dreams of becoming a published author got lost in the endless friction that parents of large families invariably drown in. Childless young couples that think they want a family should *run*, not walk, to the nearest psychiatrist.

I won't dwell on the 46 years that elapsed, but I actually began writing the first page of this Foreword on Sunday, August 15, 1999 at 2:45 a.m. to be exact. I was not and am not in the mood to be charitable, the reasons for which will become obvious as we proceed.

One of the mushrooming demands in America is for Government action *against* all forms of media that publish, illustrate, circulate, or even offer, any and all forms of "pornography" whatsoever. For the moment let's leave that dangerous bomb entirely alone. Let's first be sure there are enough kegs of powder too really blow hell out of things. Then we'll light it.

That particular observation describes one of my basic weaknesses. I always want the whole panorama in full swing right from the opening first note . . . darn all the fiddle fretting around building up to it. So please forgive me if I forget at times that you have not walked in my shoes for 80 years, and thus I may sometime assume that you feel and see and hurt with equal experience and sensations.

The whole purpose of this Foreword is to tell you that for 70 years I tried my best to be a Christian. The balance of the book is to explain how and why I failed. My only reason for writing any of it, is the hope that I can help someone else, maybe even you, to avoid wasting your life-time stumbling fruitlessly on the same path.

Stumbling along on that path, hurt and lost, should not happen to a dog.

It did not really begin on the afternoon I stood there appalled before those ancient torture devices. I'd had misgivings and un-answered questions before . . . but it was the utterly undeniable existence and purposes they had been used for that proved to me irrevocably that something was wrong with God's Church. It put in me the absolute determination to find out what that wrong was. I began looking for truth . . . .

The first truth is that I wasn't in a dungeon in Spain. I was in a dungeon beneath one of the oldest Cathedrals in London, England . . . . and in looking for the truth ever since, I have found more and more, and more lies. This book is about just some of them, for I doubt a whole library would hold all of them.

Frankly, I don't care one whit *what* people believe. That is their individual business and of no concern to me. But when a belief propels herds of them into damaging the rights and freedoms of others, when such belief continually and constantly results in hideous wars and slaughter, and when such belief is obviously destroying my country's future and its citizen's well being, *then it damned well IS my business!*

The facts, and their inevitable results, also make it *your business!* But making any decision or engaging in any action as a result of that decision, when instigated without knowing the alternatives possible, is the action of a fool.

CHAPTER ONE

"Snicker, snicker" . . . . someone just mentioned the ". . . world's oldest profession." and of course, everyone *knows* what is being referred to. But they know it only through sheer ignorance of the facts. Mass wars, fratricide, genocide, homicide, rape, and suicide stem from and occur because of the same condition. Whoring is *not* the world's oldest profession; not, in fact, by thousands of years, and at least a half dozen other professions were already firmly entrenched before the first "trick" was consummated.

P.T. Barnum wasn't the only opportunist that saw humankind as suckers just begging to be fleeced. All sorts and kinds of con-jobs are birthed every minute of every day, with no regard on the part of the "parent" for what havoc his "brat" may cause. If he makes a buck or gets the horse-laugh on the victims of his scam, vunderbar . . . his cup runneth over with joy. Thus historical fact has been dealt with cruelly in more ways than one, and certainly for many P.T. Barnum reasons . . . but . . .

Each time legitimate experts uncover more evidence, whole new concepts of the history of homosap unfold, especially his ages and origins. In the mid 70's geological evidence dated man's first appearances in the mid-Cenozoic era, or roughly 100,000 years ago. Discoveries since . . . not the Piltdown man kind . . . have moved early histories of humans back much further. Oddly enough, mentioning the age of the human race in most conversations, brings very skeptical expressions on our listeners' faces. Particularly is this so if they are Religious. Ah . . . but they one and all seem to know about and remember the Piltdown man fraud . . . thus have paid little if any attention to legitimate finds that belie great swarms of "everyone knows" type stuff.

"In the beginning . . . (Biblical) . . . nothing was created." But let's look at that idea later. It contradicts the Bible and we'd alienate millions discussing it now. Let's stick to early historical facts. For hundreds of years humans knew nothing of meat consumption and were strictly herbivorous. They knew nothing of tilling edible plants, only how to seek them in their immediate vicinity and pluck them. They are called therefore, the "gatherers." Beliefs in that long ago era were simple and practical. What ever was available was for *everyone's* use. Man, woman, or child, all went hunting and gathering whatever food plants they could find. In those simple, totally uninformed humans, was a practical and needed reality that has been destroyed. Among the realities was Sex, (that means fucking, hon). It was on a par with all else in their lives . . . *it belonged to everyone!* Man, woman, child . . . anyone that wanted to get a little had no shame or jackassing around about it. Being kin, or not being kin had no bearing either. Despite what today's up-tight moralists may preach against such modus operandi, the uninhibited sex practice of these early people is likely a major reason the human race survived, for our globe at that time was exceedingly hostile to human life. To that fact another must be added: The human was one of the most defenseless creatures in existence. No claws, no fangs, sluggish and slow in ability to flee, he was at the mercy of flora, fauna, and fortune, for Nature herself was much wilder and rawer those many centuries ago. Raw winters, burning summers, volcanoes, earthquakes, floods, raging oceans, savage jungles filled with powerful predators, plus a total lack of knowledge about anything, made of man a very unlikely candidate for survival. With no understanding or methods of treatment whatsoever, even a small scratch on his leg or arm could become fatal. But fucking was fun, just about the only fun he ever knew in his entire life. It was not forbidden for no P. T. Barnum types had yet dreamed up any Gods. (We'll discuss the sad introduction of them presently.)

Tens of thousands of years later, when the almost equally ignorant bigoted old Priests went with exploration ships into the Americas, the South Sea Islands, and other "undiscovered" habitats, they found the same conditions. Fucking was fun; it belonged to everyone; There were no taboos, hang-ups, shames, rapes, nor *any* venereal diseases. Marital strife and problems were unknown. Children really were raised by the village. Jealousy, thievery, rape, shame of one's body, all the other adverse problems facing society today were spawned in the Dark Ages of Europe when Deity Religions obliterated knowledge and common sense. Most of the gargantuan ills concerning these matters that we suffer from today were brought on by this anti-nature nonsense. That nonsense has been so thoroughly imbedded into human minds that to many millions of them it has become "truth." Dislodging the moon and setting it free, to no longer be subservient to earth's gravity, would likely be an easier task than loosing the populace from their Religious beliefs. But don't trash this book now. Dare to find out why I said that.

In the mid-1700's a man by the name of Franz (Fredrich) Anton Mesmer, an Austrian physician, discovered a crude form of hypnosis. His discovery was hooted at, ridiculed, made a plaything by writers of the day, and eventually became little more than side-show bally-hoo in cheap carnivals or acts by stage "magicians" and their trained Trilby's. Hypnosis occupied that lowly and mostly discredited status until World War II. Captured GI's, in a Japanese Prisoner of War camp, had nothing whatsoever to treat wounded or sick buddies with. In one of those suffering, afflicted groups, a doctor who was also a prisoner was faced with a young soldier whose life depended on surgery. The Jap authorities of the camp sneered at the need, would furnish nothing to help.

This doctor had read some of the "nonsense" rituals of hypnotism and was not wholly convinced one way or the other about its possible merits. In a last ditch attempt to help the suffering soldier, he tried the rituals of hypnotizing. He managed to put that young soldier into a trance, perform the needed surgery with a crude knife . . . and saved the kid's life. But the glaring truth had hit home hard. *Hypnotism worked! The soldier had NOT felt any pain or distress what ever while being cut on!*

The news was not known outside that POW camp for several years after the event. By the time the doctor could reveal it, most of the media shrugged and said "so what." But some thoughtful members of the medical profession did heed the news and some Medical research centers did begin investigating. Even though over 200 years have passed since discovery of hypnotic phenomena, very little is generally known about it. Medical Science knows very little more. The reasons are many and most of them ludicrous.

The news about the induced trance and painless surgery did get aired about to some extent. Scribes of the fourth estate did learn and write about Medical research concerning hypnotic possibilities. Writers seldom miss a bet to write something that will get published and make a buck . . . so the Bridie Murphy tales hit the book stores. Being hypnotically "regressed" to a former life became the "in" fad of the day. Thousands of people grabbed the ribbon and danced around the maypole of re-incarnation beliefs. Big bucks were made with daring "first hand, *true*" accounts of former lives. Edgar Cayce became an accepted "proof" of one leg of the craze.

In the meantime, some doctors *did* begin using hypnosis in actual surgical procedures, and for the most part, when properly administered, the results are nothing short of phenomenal. Unfortunately several things have thwarted most of the possibilities of new frontiers in the matter being adequately explored. For one thing . . . writers!

While the fad concerning hypnotism was beginning to snowball, it inspired some writers: Here indeed was publishable script. Ironically, the yarns that sell best are the ones that promote the *worst* fears. Hypnotizing *women,* WOW! They could be forced to do things (read that fucking, hon) against their will. Stage magicians with their beautiful female stooges being hypnotized and done what-ever with, helped terrorize the populace about the vulnerability of women under an unscrupulous hypnotizing fiend. Medical research in the thing became feared and brought demands for it to stop.

All of that is par for the course when science begins messing around with people. Particularly loud are the screams if the experimentations seem to confound or contradict Biblical edicts.

Unfortunately for the Priests and Preachers, nearly every thing that scientists have delved into for the last couple of centuries has wrought havoc to, directly confounds, or diametrically opposes and discredits God's "Holy" Word. Scientifically controlled investigations and research require big bucks aplenty and most experts in these fields *have to depend* on Government subsidies, big grants, etc. Thus to keep huge out-lays of dollars flowing to their cause, these harried investigators will from time to time be *forced* to issue statements to the press that they believe in, and except God as a reality. Some of them have been so contemptuous of the necessity that they have issued such non-sequiturs as: "This new discovery indicates a Supreme Being for its source." Oh yez, oh yez . . . indeed!

Another tried and true pacifier was plopped into the public's crying mouth about vulnerable women and heinous satyrs who might learn to manipulate them with hypnotism. The pacifier was quite simple. It was announced officially with a straight face: ". . . no one can be hypnotized against their will."

Writers pounced on the thing and even check-out stand tabloids crowed with the good news . . . which in itself is proof of the powers of suggestion subjugating *anyone's* will. All that's needed is an "acceptable" mantra. This one relieved the public's concern, and with slightly raised eyebrows, those investigating the nitty-gritty of hypnosis were able to continue unmolested.

Such statements are frequently a crock full . . . dipped right out of the potty.

Any successful salesman, any writer of effective advertising, any Priest or Preacher, and certainly any politician, uses the basics of hypnosis continually, or they soon have to hunt a new way to make a living. It is quite true that many people are much easier to mesmerize than others. In an audience, a competent hypnotist, preacher, politician or good salesman can quickly spot those easiest,

and also those who are hardest, to sway. A good operator ignores
the hard cases and concentrates on the vulnerable. When these
"easy marks" are mesmerized by the speaker's golden oratory, they
in turn become "convincers" of the skeptics. This is the basis of
why mobs are so easily created, and can be led to do things *none* of
them would have done otherwise.

Let's quit referring to the phenomena as hypnotism and start
calling it by a more *acceptable* identity. The term *persuasion* will
not alarm anyone. But *persuasion*, dear reader, is one of the most
powerful tools that humans have at their disposal. The bulk of
humanity is almost wholly controlled by it. Why do you buy a
Coke, or a Bud, a can of Del Monte fruit, or a pair of Nikes? Your
answer will immediately be that you bought a particular brand
because it is the best for the money. Meanwhile your next-door
neighbor swears the same thing about Pepsi, Falstaff, Libby's, or
Chevrolets. In the U.S. alone, *millions* of dollars are spent every
day telling us what to buy, use, think, or vote on. But these huge
sums are not being spent by millionaire philanthropists atoning
for their many sins by doing a public service. The whole total cost
is added to the products being touted, thus me, you, and every
one else is shelling out tons of money to be told *what* to buy, *who*
to vote for, how to be saved, cured, healed, how not to stink, and
even what to think. Particularly are we *persuaded* in what to think,
and NOT to think, *all of our entire lives in fact.*

It may be possible for a writer to make a statement that would
be more publicly and personally unacceptable than the one I just
made, but he'd have to burn a lot of mid-night oil to eventually
conceive it. So let's repeat it to be absolutely sure you didn't miss
it: *All of your whole life, uncounted billions of dollars are being spent
to hypnotize you into WHAT to think!* Yeah, and in what NOT to
think or believe too!

For the moment let's forget what happens as a fetus is
developing. We'll also ignore the multitude of limitations that
may be imposed on him from scads of things beyond his control . . .
mental ability, physical agilities, looks, (or lack of them), latent

talents, etc., etc. There are far too many and in too many variations to even understand, let alone write about. *No two children are born equal, not even identical twins!* But let's DO look for a moment at how and when this baby's hypnotizing begins. Let's just see how he is "programmed" on what to think, and on what he MUST NOT think.

By the time a newborn babe is three of four months old, if he is normal and healthy, he is vividly alert to everything near him. Groping, tiny hands will seek to grab anything that attracts him. If he can latch onto it, he doesn't stop to read the directions, just pops it into his mouth to see if it's edible. A sock, a toe, your finger, his rattler . . . anything he can grasp, gets the taste test. By this age, with proper handling, when his diaper is changed and/or he gets a nice warm bath, especially of his private parts, his exploring, inquisitive little hands find his genitalia. Instant pleasure of the contact can be seen on the cherubic little face. It takes only a few seconds of his pulling and playing with his equipment for anyone present to see definite results. He *loves the sensations!* Left alone he will begin chortling with glee while pleasuring himself with the manipulations.

Then descends calamity! Mamma is horrified. Her pleasant smile and cheerful attitude are instantly replaced with storm warnings and great displeasure. Many misguided mothers will slap the mystified babe's hand. "NO!" She'll yelp in utter horror. "Nasty! You'll hurt yourself! Don't do that!"

Even as you read this, it IS happening to thousands of tiny babies, both male and female, all over our land. While that certainly is NOT the "good news" of this particular illustration, the really *bad* news is that every darned one of those loving young mothers is convinced beyond redemption that she is doing the right thing in scolding and *forcing* her child to NOT play with himself.

When mamma goes ballistic because the child is playing with his genitalia, he is dumbfounded! Often it is the first time he has seen or heard a cross word from her. It is the first time he has experienced her wrath and displeasure, and he is totally mystified

and no little cowed. And though neither he nor she realizes it, she
has begun his brain-washing . . . his *hypnotizing* into "thinking,"
and even more importantly into NOT "thinking."

But there I go again: Wanting the entire orchestra sounding
off in full voice, their vibrant, swelling notes rattling the rafters . . .
while actually I've presented only one small violin experimentally
running a simple scale trial melody theme. Let's see if we can at
least get a flute to join in.

For one brief moment let's return to the young prisoner of war
soldier who needed surgery. Words, mere suggestive words, properly
delivered, readied him for an operation. It has since then been
learned that hypnosis can be used on human minds to perform all
sorts of painful procedures without the patient experiencing any
trauma or pain what ever. Yet the above described scene of mamma
and baby has been happening in that poor kid's family for
uncounted generations past, so drastically, that in all likelihood it
has become irremovably implanted in his DNA pattern. Since the
"persuasion" thus implanted is diametrically opposed to much of
his other DNA survival patterns, also stamped in from centuries of
survival needs, it is inevitable that he begins his life confounded
by his own needs and emotions. As he grows up he will be subjected
continually and constantly to more and more of this "Christian"
warping against "sinful" things. As a result he can seldom even
approach a rational life, or a reasonable mental attitude about that
life. Remember that far less effective "persuasion" IS being used as
the only painkiller for exceedingly painful surgery, tooth removal,
etc. Practitioners of this art can even control the patient's bleeding
while cutting, simply by "instructing" the mesmerized mind on
the table. Thus, any and all of us, should be extremely cautious
about thinking we "know" anything. Far wiser is he who boldly
questions and doubts, being very slow and reluctant to form an
"opinion" about anything, but especially "opinions" concerning
moral beliefs.

In at least a dozen essays published over the years in numerous
periodicals I have used the following, which I deem fitting to quote

here: "Opinion is the only thing known to science that can be created out of absolutely nothing. Facts, proof, and common sense are frequently its most obviously missing ingredients."

Unfortunately the babe's beginning that I have described, invariably plunges the kid into obfuscation before his life has more than just begun. Then every day of his life, "Religious" adherents will swamp him from all sides with more and more of it. "Creating" him required a mixing of opposites, male seed plus female receptacle. To enhance this, make sure it occurs, Nature over millions of years has embedded in all living things, an irresistible urge to get the union accomplished. NO life of any kind would have ever survived otherwise. It is NOT a depravity nor promiscuous behavior for a male of any species to ardently strive to implant his seeds in a female. It is his Nature, his "reason" for existence. Equally strong and compelling was the female desire to accommodate him . . . until Religion screwed up her thinking even worse than it messed up his.

When the first split off of human types began, scientists have determined that numerous types resulted. Quite a few of those various "human-like" creatures became extinct, but as with all of Nature's attempts to maintain life, some survived and became the early "gatherers." This forbearer of modern man was usually about 4 feet tall and lived a maximum of about 30 to 40 years. His brain was equally small and under developed. Though he could, and did, stand on his hind legs when necessary, much of his locomotion was accomplished by using his front "knuckles" in combination with his hind legs as he moved. Three major reasons kept him from becoming extinct also. (1.) He had opposing thumbs that made it possible for him to use his front "paws" for almost any thing he wanted to do. This gave him a marked advantage over stronger beasts of all sorts who could NOT "handle" objects. (2.) He learned that the flesh of other animals was edible. This greatly multiplied his protein intake, its chief benefits being to promote growth of his brain as well as resiliency of his physical make-up. It also increased his almost constant need for sex. Selective? Indeed!

Any female available and willing, any time, and any place. Beginning at an early age, both genders became not only willing, but also eager for the experience.

People now will consider it extremely gross, but as humans learned to eat meat, their own kind was discovered to be quite tasty too. Cannibalism became one of the earliest human practices. It had far reaching effects then, and still does today.

In any human settlement of any kind, today as well as in the beginning of our species, some individuals fare better than others. Always there are those who can see, think, and do better than their brothers. Throughout history these special ones have become leaders, advisors, and/or the ones copied and envied. In those very uninformed early people, those who stood out in abilities of survival and were able to find the best pickings, just naturally became "leaders" whom the rest of the clan tried to follow. So that the real truth is, the world's "oldest" profession is being the "leader." From "leader" he rapidly developed into being the boss, or "King."

But the ones with special talents for "finding," or "doing," (or at least being mistaken by the rest of the clan as to having those qualities) are not always the smartest. Throughout history, in any group of people anywhere, there are always one or two who can and do think rings around all the others. As this individual gains age and experience, many of the "tribe" will begin seeking his advice or guidance. It was inevitable that this type person became practitioner of the "Second" oldest profession . . ."Advisor." Being "King" or "Advisor" is time consuming. Neither job could be done well if the one doing it had to spend most of his time gathering food. It took neither of them very long to convince the rest of the tribe, that if they wanted real leadership, safety, and advice, then those seeking it had to supply the leaders with the food they needed. Supporting these two "oldest" professionals instigated the first "tax" system.

Keeping always in mind that we are examining small tribes of "people" who were very little advanced over monkeys, it is easy to understand the gradual development that occurred. Perhaps one day the group encountered a beast of prey smack in the middle of their berry patch. The "followers" would expect the King to do something. He would in turn, as "Leaders" of today still do, look to the "Advisor" for ideas. This worthy does NOT want to give up the easy job with all the free groceries. So . . . he grabs a dry piece of brush. Shaking it to create a threatening rustle, he charges at the beast, yelling and raising hell. Beasts of all kinds, then and now, are easily alarmed by sudden actions from creatures they know nothing of . . . and mankind has always fit this category with nearly all beasts. The predator growled threateningly even as he fled . . . but he DID go. The "Advisor" thus heaped upon himself much acclaim and trust.

A few days later, while the tribe is peacefully filling their bellies with ripe berries, there looms out of nowhere, a sudden violent storm. Howling winds, ominous broiling clouds threaten . . . and all of a sudden a smashing bolt of lightening slams into a huge tree near by, splitting it from top to bottom and leaving a smoking, smoldering mess of what an instant before had been a living, healthy giant. The tribe is terrified. Fearfully they look to the King for protection. Guess who he turned to.

The one chosen as "advisor" would likely have been one who had been around longer than most of the other tribe members. He had gained "experience" most of them had not yet undergone. Experience was then, and is now, still the best teacher. The bush shaking and yelling had scared off a vicious beast . . . what if . . . ? And, scared of the streaking, howling pandemonium around him, he grabbed the self same bush, shook it at the roaring storm. Shaking that bush, he charged at the roaring tumult, yelling mightily back at it. And though the great storm continued to grumble and growl, it too was subsiding and leaving. No one in the tribe got knocked into the next county by lightening and as the "Advisor" continued his gymnastics, the storm receded.

The tribe, in the space of just a few days, had seen evil personified, driven away by the "Advisor." And so was born the first "incantation." It was a "protection" against the "evils" that threatened them on all sides. The "Advisor" had gained kudos galore, and it is very probable that he had also convinced himself of his "magical" powers. Quite naturally he would become a very revered person, and the balance of the tribe would believe in him and his "power" with little if any reservations.

Is it hard to imagine that sometimes the "Power" might not work? Suppose, that under dire threat and danger from some natural "enemy" of the tribe, that the "incantations" didn't work and the tribe suffered a grievous loss? Faith and trust in the "King" and/or his "Advisor" would wither and the tribe in its grief and fear might well turn on either or both of the leaders. They had been chosen because of their "ability" to think and to act. It would not take "a leader" very long to understand that he needed protection when things went wrong. Nor would it take very long to find two or three of the strongest men in the tribe who wouldn't mind getting free groceries themselves. Most of the time their "work" would consist of merely being close to the King and/or his Advisor. Their mere presence as "protector" would be quite enough to keep King and Advisor safe in normal times. In the event of leadership, advice, or incantation failure, knocking a few heads lopsided is small problem to many of the muscle types anyway.

Naturally, these "muscles" would need free groceries too. They could do little protecting while in the field plucking their own berries.

In that need arose one of the first real problems with "government." The tribe is already working their butts off feeding themselves and their King/Advisor leaders. They most certainly would NOT be in favor of adding to their load just to protect the two leaders from themselves! Already many in the tribe might not be in total agreement with the duo anyhow. The solution is one of the first principles of herd control. Give them a *motivation*, a *reason* to agree to more taxation and thus additional "government." Government, of any size or in any era, has always meant "subservience" for those being governed. It may have happened like this:

One day the tribe went to its favorite berry patch and found it already stripped of all the ripe berries. A neighboring tribe was just leaving, loaded with loot from the vines, and the ones who usually gathered their food there were out of luck, and food.

"We need *protection* from those *apes!*" the King roared in his most convincing and Kingly manner. But please note well the dual *persuasion* gimmick here. Protection of self is powerful motive with anyone. A King can sell that with relative ease. In and of itself however, it will raise only limited support. To really control the village, a leader *must present* a whipping boy, someone the tribe will hate as well as fear. In the case we are examining, it is ". . . those *apes!*" NO endorsement of any cause can be very successful with out that all-important "enemy" for everyone to hate and fear. Giving an enemy a "tag" that will instantly fan hate in the populace is vital. The most careful and thorough study of human history can find NO conflict between tribes, Nations, or races, that has *ever* been waged *without* those two vital necessities, hate and fear!

Politics have never changed since that earliest beginning; they have only evolved to become more subtly evil. Any and all great "programs" that need much loot (taxes) to mount and maintain, still must use those two prime basic principles: (1.) Self Protection, (or self aggrandizement) and (2.) a whipping boy." Today, even as you read this, we are being bilked out of uncounted billions of dollars to support God only knows how many "programs" launched and maintained by our own "Kings." Not a darned one of those costly programs could have been instigated and financed without the two prime motivations we're discussing. No war would, or could, ever have been fought without very heavy application of these two gimmicks by the "Kings" and "Advisors" of *both* sides. How very like those first crude human types we still are! And as P.T. Barnum said: "There's one (a sucker) born every minute."

A few lines back it was stated: "not everyone in the village fully agreed with the Leader or Advisor." With no doubt what ever, this has occurred in all societies, and under all governments throughout the entire history of human kind. For tens of thousands of years, the "dissenters" were usually under a regime where in they had to strictly keep their objections in the closet or suffer dire consequences. Little by little these malcontents find each other and frequently start underground movements. Such movements can grow strong enough to topple an Empire. More frequently they have gotten their "members" heavily penalized, up to and including being hung or boiled in oil.

So continually have these "dissenter" movements come about in Governments, in Societies, in Religions, and in "Beliefs" that it is high time someone gave a name to the phenomena. I choose here and now to name it "The Great Dual Society." Ideally it should have membership cards, awards, meetings, rituals, and great recognition. Actually, very few people exist that don't belong to it in some respect, but all too often will not, or perhaps *cannot* admit it, frequently not even to themselves.

Human inability to admit or face being "dual" in belief or practice is most prevalent in the membership of Religious "isms." Religious bigotry has conceived "moral" concepts, and has even managed to turn many of them into LAWS enforced by government. But, since *natural* practices by humans, which is *demanded* by Nature herself, is, and always has been very gross "sin" with the churches, many of their members covertly engage in sexual activities outside of wedlock, but simply refuse to face it honestly and intelligently. Membership in just this one part of The Great Dual Society is *very* numerous indeed.

The Great Dual Society has existed for the entire history of humankind. One would think that the chief cause for its existence was Government opposition. All Governments of every kind have all had dissenters, even though the misgivings usually had to be kept under cover. But it can be shown that of all movements ever created on the face of this earth, Religions have caused more problems than any other. Showing this to be true is somewhat involved and complicated. Of necessity we must look at some of the history of religions. But we must look much further than the "everyone knows" type stuff, for most of that was created by the

Religions themselves. Remember that Churches in no manner what ever can allow themselves to be discredited where their version of "truth," God, and Righteousness are concerned. For a Church, its tenets, or practices to be suspected of falseness, is to sign a death warrant for it. For survival, Religions, for reasons, and by actions we will explore as we proceed, have caused the greatest hoaxes ever perpetrated on mankind. Ridiculously, the results of that have adversely affected the human race more than any other misfortune that has ever occurred to us, bar none.

But there is a quality, or an ability, let's say a "proclivity" about the human mind that is tip-toed around very carefully by most of the scientific experts. Indeed at times humans seem "hard wired" to needs, feelings, or compulsions the sum of which is greater than the component parts of what we actually know. Seemingly working against thousands of religious beliefs, a hidden, but strident "inner self" dictates demands from Nature with her constant admonition to "reproduce." Diametrically opposed to this "inner self" and its almost constant sexual demands, stands the "taught to us" *conviction* of a Colossus, a grim, totalitarian despot who says "Thou shalt not! Or I'll burn your soul in Hell Fire forever!" Proof wise, this "Godly" order is as bogus as any scam ever perpetrated by man, but is never the less a force of formidable power indeed!

People by the millions have been raised, right from their mamma's first yelp about her baby grabbing its little genitalia, into an *unhealthy* belief in God. Thousands of our people rarely if ever go to church . . . yet will NOT denounce their "belief" of that God. Thousands who regularly go to church have never really read the Bible, and know almost nothing about the true history of their Religion, or of Religions in general. Never the less, they have, over the decades since our Government was first formed, passed countless laws based on Religious ideals and prohibitions. And there in hinges a very great wrong, a curtailment of human nature that is inanely ludicrous. Not only have we saddled ourselves with illogical laws that are constantly broken and exploited by many thousands of us, but we have also dictated for ourselves lives we cannot comfortably live. To escape the idiocy of this crunch we are subservient to, we become members of the Great Dual Society, although most usually strictly on the Q.T. There is no way to even estimate how many countless millions of lives have been made bad jokes of, or how many people have been utterly destroyed by this unfortunate duplicity.

It begins with mamma's first scolding of baby when he/she grabs little genitalia. Then through a life time of "moral" deceit, insisted on by our Religiously oriented peers, laws, and brainwashing, the unworkable and unenforceable "unnaturalness" of the "beliefs" cause deprivation, curtailment of human rights, needs, and abilities to ridiculous degrees, not infrequently finishing its toll on a victim in the trauma center of a Hospital or in the penitentiary. The cloaks it wears are called Religions, Righteousness with God . . . faith . . . . Salvation . . . . virginity . . . . celibacy . . . Oh yes, or burn in Hell forever!

. . . . and in truth all of these are the biggest and most harmful LIE ever conceived!

Even while you read this, the LIE, the Hoax, is cheating YOU. It has cheated you all the days of your life and is the direct (and also the indirect) cause of most of your problems in this life. If you have courage enough to read this book and let your "inner self" come alive, the very least you will gain is freedom and peace of mind. This is something NO Christian has ever really had, or ever will have if he has any mind left at all. The best any of them have ever achieved is being *mesmerized*. Yes, *hypnotized*, just as if a skilled surgeon was preparing them for painless surgery.

So long and with such infallible methods have we been hypnotized by "God Beliefs," that we cannot even imagine or believe the restraints, and "unnatural" existence we have been hoaxed into. All of us are victims. The condition is inescapable in a Society dominated by minds so Religiously corrupted that most of them long ago were rendered incapable of thinking clearly or intelligently about their beliefs and their harmful tenets. But most certainly are we victims when alternate opinions to the "accepted" ones can not be heard . . . or even "discussed" for that matter. If this seems an extravagant statement, announce in your own bailiwick that you have become a convinced atheist, and prepare to be ostracized totally, even by long standing friends and kinfolks. The hell of it is, that even those who ostracize you, will most likely be members of the Great Dual Society themselves, albeit usually totally unable to believe or be convinced themselves of how great is their own perfidy and rationalization.

In the following chapters I'll invite you to take a cold hard look at the biggest potpourri of herd deception ever perpetrated by humans on humans, anywhere. It is all around you everywhere. When you begin to see the web, and the tenacious ways it has been woven, you will discover that you, yes, YOU have been ensnared in it for your entire life. Escape is not easy, nor will it be painless. But it *can be accomplished* if you have the nerve to try, and the mental ability to think.

CHAPTER TWO

Making a bold statement of an "alleged" fact that is generally unknown, therefore suspicious at best, regardless of how well conceived it might be, is the shortest distance between two points of non-acceptance in a sea of human "quasi-thinking." Particularly is this true if the "fact" contradicts accepted beliefs. Instant rejection for that kind of idea is usual with most people. To achieve any semblance of acceptance for an unknown new concept, a path must first be blazed through many muddled misconceptions already accepted by the public. To wipe away some of the Smog of our Societal Concepts and define The Great Dual Society as it exists, so that its reality might be more clearly seen, let's begin by going back a few years. But when I say a "few" years, I realize that the era we'll first visit was well before many of you were born. Take my word for it, that is a very, very *few* years . . . so few in fact, that it seems like yesterday. It was 1926 and I was 5 years old . . . .

"Yours and mine's different," she insisted. She was almost 6, not yet old enough to begin 1st grade in Texas at that time.

"Hungh?" I still wasn't sure what she meant about our "things" being different.

"They just are. I'll show you."

"uh . . . awright."

"But if I show you mine, you gotta show me yours."

"uh . . . awright."

By the side of the house, in a space where there was no window, she sat on the ground and pulled her small panty leg aside . . . and what do you know . . . . *hers was different!*

It may seem a bit odd now, but . . . looking at hers, she showing it unhampered by any other consideration except not being caught at it by grown-ups, I experienced no shame or reluctance in showing her mine. Nor was mine quite as easy to expose, since I had not only a pair of short pants on, but also underwear. She finally wound up helping me, and her small warm hand grasping my little penis to get it out into view was the most eerie and pleasing sensation I had ever experienced. She didn't let go, fingered it, turned it this way and that . . . and then to my utter inability to explain, she posed a question:

"Is it fun to pee out of?"

"Uh . . . . I dunno what you mean?"

"Mine's not. I have to sit down. You can stand up, hold yours in your hand and squirt it like a hose."

"uh . . ."

"I bet that's fun."

"uh . . ."

"Nobody can see us here. Stand up and pee a little . . . and let me hold it while you do."

"uh . . ."

"I'll let you feel of mine if you will."

I peed for her. I tingled when she put my hand on her vagina. I tingled when she put her hand on my penis. I know now that she must have had some prior experience, perhaps with her brother who was a year or so older than she. For she, throughout that memorable day, and on many occasions later, *knew* things her parents hadn't taught her. I wanted, I really *needed*, to investigate, handle, and explore her equipment a very great deal more than I had nerve enough to even suggest, let alone achieve.

A thousand, thousand scenes I clearly recall, from all the years of my life, each and all of them proving that current "morals" demanding segregation of kids from sex is a gargantuan mistake and a lie. But, though we will presently consider more events and proof, I must at this time pause and wonder: Am I the only human who can remember pre-puberty quandaries concerning the physical body of "the other gender?" Who answered our questions? Who gave us intelligent answers to the things we needed, actually hurt to know? Who explained and erased inhibitions and cover-ups? Does there really exist a kid of 6 or 7 who doesn't have built in curiosities about what's under "all them clothes" of the other gender?" I can't believe very many exist who aren't eaten alive by those needs! But most kids are being hamstrung, badgered, and lied to from a very early age, actually *forcing* them to dodge, evade, hide, and go underground with all their needs and questions, to get what answers they can from anywhere and anyone, except the ones they should be able to depend on . . . their own parents! And their own teachers! That's the same thing I had to do in that long ago, God besotted era. We'll investigate fully, why unnatural and perverse remedies are the only recourse for these kids. And when we clearly spotlight the answers, we'll have a beginning understanding of what is wrong with the scenes and the people in America today . . . .

Yes! I mean school shootings, thousands of teen pregnancies out of wed-lock, our over-crowded prisons, gargantuan numbers of drug and/or alcoholic casualties, the "don't give a damn" attitude of our young, and the heartbreak of suicides of young people who'd not yet even begun to live. "Whoa!" you say? How can I jump from a couple of little kids playing "show me" to a hoodlum in jail for peddling dope or raping someone? Go back into your memory and stroll around for a moment. When, where, and from whom, did YOU learn the word *fuck?* When, where and from whom were you informed about what fucking involved? At what age did you begin masturbating? And why did you? Then be as honest as possible with this one: Did your mother and/or father teach YOU all of these things you learned? Or, like me, did you learn them from other kids you played with? I had to learn them literally from the gutter! There was no other source willing to teach me.

When mama first shows displeasure at baby's playing with his genitalia, he quickly learns NOT to do it when she can see. That does NOT keep him from investigating the pleasurable feeling when she ISN'T around. The little six year old girl had already learned to find a place no grown-ups could see to further "investigate" penises and have her own "difference" examined. Presently I'll describe how I first learned about "fucking." But the point in all of this should already be apparent. At age five I had already been ushered into the Great Dual Society, the by-laws of which are "hide what you want to do from the world around you and DO it!"

Think about "persuasion." The bulk of our populace has been "persuaded" to believe that fucking is an abomination to God. Therefore our "persuaded" Society reeks with attempts to curtail all activity, education, investigation, discussion, and/or reference to the procedure. Even pictures of nudes are verboten! So what happens? Nature knows no God! Nor does she heed ANY of his "commandments." She instills in all living things an overpowering need, a drive to reproduce. What we have as a result is an irresistible force meeting an immovable absurdity. No Government, no laws, no punishment, however cruel and severe, and no God, has *ever* been able to stop all the out of wedlock fucking going on. No amount of unwanted results from the act has ever kept it from happening either. The dire threat of an eternity in hell hasn't stopped it for the last 2000 years. Yahweh couldn't stop it for thousands of years before that. Isn't it high time we began trying to treat the act, and information about it, with something besides Religiously "persuaded" absurdities? "Religious Hypnotism" invariably seems to beget *stupidity!*

Today, millions of dollars are being contributed to and spent by Church Groups, and the supposedly "concerned citizen" groups, to thwart and prevent sex education for school children. Gargantuan pressure is being brought on lawmakers and school leaders alike to teach "abstinence" only, or at least as the "better" alternative. Damned few of the parents involved in these demands, even those who insist that it is a "parent's" right to teach his child about sex, have any ability or nerve at all to teach their kids anything about sex whatsoever. Most of them are shame faced and abashed at any attempt to discuss it with their kids, and wind up procrastinating until the kid has already learned from the streets, washrooms, and the gutter.

These same misguided ("hypnotized") herds diligently fight "Planned Parenthood" activities nation wide and blame the materials and information used by the Planners for most of the teenage sex that is happening. Here again is proof of my statement that humans don't live long enough to get any real perspective about anything. The identical per capita out of wed-lock fucking happened when I was a teenager, as is happening now, but there were many more reasons to keep it quiet: Shotgun weddings were NOT fantasy fiction, nor did "Family Planning" groups exist. There was also a lot more cuckolding going down than any husband of that era wanted to know about. If cuckolding caused fatal heart attacks on the husbands of errant wives, the human race would not today be numbering six billion people. If "cheating" husbands died as "punishment" for their sexual "sins," the human race would be extinct. When will we grow up enough to face facts? Someone really should inform the Churches. Fucking is here to stay.

The Great "Moral" Majority, "persuaded" all the days of their lives that sex should be hush-hush stuff we all should try to pretend doesn't exist, also bring great pressure onto law-makers, judges, and police to outlaw and ban any and all media presentation of nudity and/or sexual portrayals. Hundreds of books, many of them by our outstanding authors, songs, movies, *all* so called "pornography," magazines such as Playboy, Penthouse, Hustler, etc., ALL of these things they have continually tried to outlaw. Failing that because of the protection of our 1st Amendment, they then took up the hue and cry to "Protect the Children" from it. Well even our judges are too brainwashed with Religious Hokum to extend constitutional rights to kids.

"Protect" them indeed!

Because of this "protection" razzle-dazzle nonsense, Kids are barred out of movies that contain even sexual suggestiveness. "Moralists" have forced moviemakers to create a rating system so the law and parents can keep kids "safe" from them. Violence is verboten too. TV is under tremendous pressure even about "questionable" displays. But with TV and movies alike, far more clamor is raised against nudity and sexual situations than about violence, dope, and crime. Kids are literally *forced* to turn to the streets, washrooms, and gutter type information available there, for any and all of their great curiosities about sex. The unavoidable "misinformation" learned and practiced there has cheapened and deteriorated sex activities as well as women to a very harmful and deplorable depth. Sex actually IS human kinds' most beautiful and enjoyable ability. But because of continual persecution, cover-up, and misinformation about it, Religious bigotry has succeeded in turning it into filth and depravity. Millions of minds in our country, particularly in our women, have become so firmly convinced about the filth and depravities of sex, that they have irreparably damaged their own sexuality, as well as their mental, moral, and physical health. Many doctors, psychiatrists, and psychologists have become aware of these problems in their patients, and the causes . . . but are forced to refrain from trying to undo the cause. For them to attempt to explain to some up-tight, frustrated, suffering woman that the roots of her problem are buried in sexual misunderstanding and starvation, sheesh . . . they would be committing career suicide.

In the past couple of decades, a few young practitioners *have* attempted to do just that. Far more often than not, their actions result in outraged letters to Ann Landers, malpractice suits in court, loss of credibility and/or license to practice in their State. Ann Landers invariably sides with the frustrated female that is complaining, and urges all her readers to immediately report *any such "depraved" person to the authorities.* Ann Landers was raised (and brain-damaged) in the same God Besotted era that I was, only she has never had the mental ability to recognize and escape her warping from it.

We have spent uncounted millions of dollars for many decades "protecting" children from all knowledge and information about sex and nudity. Movies and television are forced to bar kids from seeing even mild productions of either. What are the results of this "protection?" Kids who are barred out of the "sexual situation" movies are getting each other pregnant. Over half of our new babies are born to women who are single, a staggering number of them not old enough to vote. Kids who aren't allowed into a movie with violence in it are stealing their father's guns and shooting up their schoolmates and teachers. Heavy dope scenes in movies also get the rating that keeps youngsters out . . . so thousands of these kids are already hooked on dope, and/or alcohol. Every day many of these kids are busted for helping peddle the stuff.

Of all first world Nations, America is the most Bible toting, Clergy infested, Church building/attending, Alcohol/dope consuming, bastard* producing Nation anywhere. We also lead the world in crimes, criminals, and prison inmates. The more our "Religious" purists have demanded and gotten laws based on Biblical "morality," the more the morals and practices of our Nation have deteriorated. (* Bastard is no longer politically correct for the child of an unwed mother. It never should have been in the first place. But you can thank God's "mercy," and his "wisdom" for the uncouthness and unfairness of it. At least three places in the Bible state with no equivocation that bastards can in no wise ever enter heaven.)

Since I have inferred that our Religious afflictions here have resulted in our being the leading cesspool for corruptness, we will use the most authoritative proof possible for consideration. In a series of tests, when the same conditions apply to each test, the results will invariably repeat themselves. This truth has become a cornerstone for scientific investigation. It is a disaster that the human race has never learned to apply this tried and proven format to our own problems, for it has already been adequately proved that ignorance of our history dooms us to have to repeat it.

In the following chapters we'll consider thumb nail sketches of the history of several giant sized Religions, the conditions those movements caused, and what they are doing to the people who still ardently follow them today. One of the things such an excursion will make vividly clear is just how gross and harmful mindlessly clinging to a Religion, any religion, will become to the Society it enslaves. But I hope it will become also vividly clear to you that ALL religions are merely identical left over hash, saved and evolved from earlier beliefs and practices, going right back to the original practice of "incantations" against dangers by the "advisor" of totally uninformed savages. You will also note that the bizarre practice of cannibalism has been carried right down to today's hypnotized "Christian" congregations. It has survived through at least a half dozen religions, right from earliest man's beliefs. Today it is called "Holy Communion."

I hope the sketches show you irrevocably that Christianity is merely another blob of left-over-ice-box hash, and IS indeed producing identical results in America that have been repeatedly disastrous for centuries in other nations. People, by the uncounted tens of millions, have been the ones who suffered from following any and all of those unworkable and unreasonable Deity beliefs. Now, people by the millions are setting the stage for a tragic repeat of those results right here in America today, for the same identical conditions are being forced on us . . . and thus will have identical results.

CHAPTER 3

Everyone is aware that there is more than one major religion in the world, but few people realize how many, nor do they understand the similarities or the significance of those facts. Worse still is lack of knowledge as to how many different Gods and Religions have swayed humanity almost from its beginning. However, perhaps the most harmful lack of all, is knowledge of the provable facts of what those religions, all of them, have caused their faithful and countless others to endure. Just for a moment take a look at the major ones of today: Hinduism, Buddhism, Jainism, Confucianism, Taoism, Shinto, Judaism, Christianity, Islam, Zoroastrianism, Zen Buddhism . . . really! Is there any need to go on? Even so, enumerating just these eleven is not a drop in the bucket compared to all the religions of the past, nor have we even mentioned Devil Worship and hundreds of varieties of Voodoo, a sea of Mediums and assorted "Spiritualists," nor any of the Gods of ancient mythologies. Basically, *all* religions from their earliest beginnings were never anything but "invented" ways to control people. P.T. Barnum types have existed in all eras in all Societies, and most likely always will. The amount of wealth this has bilked from the "faithful" over the centuries, or even what it is getting today, is incalculable.

It would require a sizeable shelf full of books to depict the workings, intricacies, and histories of just the 11 major religions named above. But quick thumbnails of just a few of them will demonstrate some truths that will condemn all religions for being the hare-brained nincompoopery they are. Actually, the power of any Religion is akin to the power a magician holds over his audience. Once the audience knows how a magician's trick is done, the performance is no longer exciting or even interesting. Farces never are interesting once the truth behind them is known and we can no longer be fooled. There is a stronger point to consider. The provable facts of what has happened to each of the nations of people who have been mesmerized into following Deity religions are nothing short of stark tragedy. Of greatest interest to America *should* be the fact that identical symptoms heralding oncoming calamities in those nations, are now overtly apparent in our own midst. In short, our people are already experiencing the same early warnings, caused by and for the exact same reasons of past blood baths, but are hell-bent-for-Georgia egging the mess on.

As a beginning to understanding the certainty of this we can first look at a general summation of earth's religions, all of them . . . for however diversified and different in age or Gods they may be, there is an uncanny sameness to all of them. Generally speaking, except for a few wise philosophers who began to suspect the truth over the centuries and guardedly tried to explain it in their writings, no real headway to understanding the truth of how religions originated was accomplished until the latter of the 1800's began ushering in the means of finding out. Archaeology, paleography, and kindred sciences began unraveling the truth from digging up long ago old cities and kingdoms. Learning to read the facts discovered from those long ago old places *should* have broken the strangle hold that religions have dominated humanity with for centuries. Unfortunately, three things have kept this from happening. (1.) Very few people bother to read dry as dust non-fiction books. Heavy non-fiction-books that don't deal with pop-culture "in" subjects are a staggering bore to everyone except scholarly types pursuing specialized enlightenment. (2.) For centuries each generation has embedded religious "persuasion" so deeply into its progeny that a majority of them are forever unapproachable with any thing whatsoever that contradicts their brainwashed opinions concerning "God." Even people who rarely, or never, go to church, will NOT stand up and be counted as "non-believers." (3.) Another fact that will be about as popular as athlete's foot and bad breath combined, is that lower I.Q. types, which incidentally is by far the majority of people, are the most adamantly and unshakably convinced about their "belief." And typically, they are also the easiest to recruit with "mystical" foofaraw.

These three "immovable" realities stand in truth's way continually and have been the major weakness that has allowed Deity religions to flourish for almost the entire history of our species. Many centuries before "religions" came into being, there was superstition, ignorance, and the fears they bred. Early humans had NO valid information about anything, but were one step higher than monkeys in that they were "aware." Awareness seeks answers, especially to avoid dangers. Explanations offered "spirits." Spirits demanded subservience. And thus Deity Religions were born.

Men who aspired to "leading" and/or "controlling" others gradually began putting superstitions and fears into groups with "protective" rituals against them. These rituals required users to assure "protection" from the evils by "sacrificing" to the "spirits" being sought, or placated. And of course the sacrifices were most usually loot for the "advisors" who were teaching and "helping" the beseechers. As centuries passed, and the "advisor" positions passed from one generation to the next, new blood and experience gradually increased and "improved" the most effective of the rituals and sacrifices. By effective we mean those that most impressed the people, and that they accepted and catered to strongest. One of the earliest of these was cannibalism. For centuries it became "truth" to the primitives, that to eat the brains of another, the victim's mental abilities would be passed on to the diner. Likewise his strength could be gained from his muscles, and of course there was the victim's genitalia for sexual power. From this, sex acts became ritualistic for some tribes. Blood sacrifices grew out of the slaughter of other humans for food.

These earliest beginnings were well before the time methods of writing were developed. The rituals and "laws" governing them were word of mouth hand me downs from one generation of "advisors" to the next. A great part of the lore on these rituals would be adopted from neighboring tribes, and even from those at war with each other. As the strongest of these groupings of rituals and beliefs controlled more and more of the ever growing populations of tribes, the people, even some of the "advisors" began to regard them as "sacred," inspired and handed down from unseen "spirits." The "spirits" became "holy," and those doing the rituals with most ardent fervor were "blessed." "Religions" had been born and now were "evolving."

It is easy to see then why a "spirit" world would so nearly resemble a tribe on earth. That was the only thing "advisors" knew to copy from and explain. It was also the only type structure the tribes could understand. The spirit world would have to also have a "leader," and of course he would be extra special in "power" and ability. This is overtly apparent in "Religious" writings such as "I am a jealous God . . ." etc., etc., *human* traits all. When one reads any of the Holy Writings describing *any* of the Gods, these *human* identities and qualifications are always present. When one reads "Holy" scripture from any of the world's religious writings, the "God" that is described, matches exactly the human Kings that ruled on Earth: Childish, self aggrandizing, temperamental, picayunish, demanding, conceited, and merciless . . . always ready with "reward" offered for those who will literally kiss his ass, *if* they do it in a manner that pleases him; but dire punishment for those who do it wrong. So now hear the words of the Lord:

HINDUISM:

Hinduism was likely the first religion to have a Trinity as its God: Brahma, the *creator;* Vishnu, the *Preserver;* and Shiva, the *Destroyer.* This precedes the Judaeo-Christian Trinity by many centuries. Time of each phase of the world to Hindus is measured in billions of years, then Shiva destroys it all. Brahma recreates it and the cycle begins again, a re-run of billions of years, over and over, ad infinitum. One's soul never dies. It dons a human body like one puts on a suit of clothes, lives out its allotted time on earth, then casts the worn "clothing" aside, to return again and again for another term of seeking perfection of itself. The mistakes, wrong doings, and failures it makes are called *karma*. These must be atoned for and nullified in future lives, and the poor soul can never escape the cycle nor find peace, *nirvana*, until he has fully atoned for all past karma and learned to live a perfect life as a human.

The Trinity of Hinduism, Brahma, Vishnu, and Shiva, are each a part of the *Universal Spirit*, Brahman, which means the World Soul. This World Soul, a three in one God (*Trimutri*) is not separate, one from the other, although they are different. They are considered different aspects or manifestations of the same divine Unity. There are a great number of additional attributes of the Triad which have been symbolized and they are also called Gods. But obviously, God to Hindus does not have the same meaning as is usual in other religions. Just one of the differences is that Brahman neither loves nor hates, does not compensate or punish, nor does he have any other anthropomorphic characteristics. In this respect Brahman is indeed different from the generally believed in "Gods" of other religions.

At each new re-creation, Brahma the Creator, creates the first man, named Manu. Out of Manu's head comes the best and holiest people. They are called Brahmins. Out of Manu's hands come the rulers and warriors. They are called *Kshatriyas*. Out of Manu's thighs come the craftsmen of the world called *Vaisyas*. And out of Manu's feet come the rest of the people, called *Sudras*. Brahma the *Creator* has thus determined that there will be four different castes of people. (Note to arm-chair philosophers who like to ponder the inexplicable: During the 1900's medical research discovered that all of human kind has only *FOUR* blood types!)

Since the chief God of Hinduism neither loves nor hates, does not reward nor punish, Hinduism has always been highly tolerant of other Religious beliefs. There is considerable admitting in their own Holy writings and accepted history that Hinduism has thus incorporated into its own religious formulas many bits and pieces from others. That is a far cry from Judaism, Christianity, or Islam claims, and is vastly different from them. As we shall presently investigate, those three religions are crammed full of alien concepts from a multitude of other races, regions, and religions . . . claiming them as their own God's edicts. At least Hinduism is more honest in this respect.

An interesting bit of trivia about Hinduism is the colorful way of explaining how long one cycle of "creation" is. It is shown in this manner: A hole a mile wide, a mile long, and a mile deep, filled with very fine hair, is the symbolic example. If one hair is removed each hundredth year, the length of time it takes to completely empty the pit is the length of one of earth's existences.

No one could marry above or below their caste status. Regardless of how many times one was reincarnated, he never escaped his own assigned caste, however oppressive or offensive to him it might be. Over the centuries the four castes began to be split in sub-divisions, or in other words can do's and can't do's in graded formats with-in each of the main divisions. The haves had plenty; the have nots, which were the bulk of the populace, had bare existence, and that only from hard labor for low pay.

There began to happen in their midst a thing I hope my reader will not miss. It would seem that if we are assured that life will never end, that we can come time and again and know that death is but a restful little nap and we can soon play again, then what the heck. Devil take the hind-most! Let's all have a ball.

It didn't work out that way.

All but the highest caste in India began to see their-selves as *trapped!* They were trapped forever to toil and slave endless hours for a bare pittance of a living. Nor could they ever escape the karma. Any of them could plainly see that far from atoning for past mistakes and "sins," that in reality they were stacking up more and more of it every day of their lives. Instead of being an "asset," the belief in reincarnation became a sentence to an eternal world hell.

Not surprisingly to those who observe and think, the

unbearable horror of endless eternities of karma did not deter Nature in her drives. Sex happens regardless of the God's laws, or Government's laws against it. There arose a multitude of "bastards" from the strictly forbidden and secretive mixing of various castes. Bastards were not allowed nor recognized by law or by Hinduism. Since the castes were already in a chaos of sub-dividing, these illegal, unplanned, and unwanted thousands became still another classification: The Out-castes, or to the "devout" they became the "untouchables." They got this wholly unfair treatment, even from the lowest and most overworked and deprived caste, the Sudras. And true to the reality of sex and Nature, they became the most numerous, literally millions of them. It became their lot to try to eke out a living any way they could, with any of the foul, undesirable tasks even the Sudras shunned. Thievery became rampant and almost totally uncontrollable. Wanton murder, rape, and crimes of all sorts became common place, nor was it only the "untouchables" who were responsible for all of it.

Into this unsavory mess came a man who had his brief hour of fame. His name was Mahatma Gandhi. In early life Gandhi understood the unfairness and foolishness of the caste system. He spent most of his adult life in very colorful and widely publicized demonstrations against the system, trying with all the cunning of the very shrewd and aware, to wake up his fellow man. He became a real saint to the outcastes and Sudras, none of who had any hope and no respite from accepted "practice." Government under the ruling caste was very powerful, but they were a decided minority. Thus India was in violent turmoil for over 50 years in the hopeless fight. An assassin, most likely hired and paid, finished Gandhi's fight . . . and the losers were the people.

One of the ritualistic practices of Hinduism was a very involved series of positions and silent mantras known as the Yogas. The Yogas and belief in reincarnation spread all over most of the world. This was not in the dark ages or anywhere near as remote to our own times. During the 1950's and 60's, right here in America, the practice of Yoga became widely accepted and attempted. Thousands of people of all ages and incomes begin trying to assume the "Lotus" position and transcend to higher realms of understanding and existence. When this book is published I will be lambasted, ridiculed and cursed for this observation: But when you get down to facts, Yoga is only another form of self "hypnosis." You can, if successful with the silent mantras, "transcend" your self to any pipe dream you wish. That is a statement and a condition we will get back to after we have a better overall view of what religions do to people.

Mahatma Gandhi's painful experience in trying to break "Religious" chains on his fellow man was not by any means unique in history. Certainly it, and the adverse conditions the populace was being drowned in were NOT unique to that one religion, nor in that one era. Identical conditions and problems occurred in India centuries earlier, and for the same reasons. In fact, the same widely occurring disillusionment, illicit fucking, bastard kids, unexplained murders, rapes, thievery et all, had mushroomed to unbearable proportion there some 2500 years ago. But as is usual, the ruling class, the Brahmins, were almost totally unaware and/or unconcerned. And then, a child was born.

BUDDHISM:

When I began planning this book I had no intentions of getting involved with religious beliefs other than those that sponsored an all Powerful God . . . Deity Religions only. But then I began to see identical parallels in the reactions of the followers to *any* successfully launched "religious" belief or practices. It will become apparent to my reader as we go, but as an all-inclusive observation, we can say here now, that ALL religions, whether led by an all-powerful "God," or merely consisting of "mental" gymnastics, invariably result in identical chaos, confusion, and wide-spread havoc. Far from *solving* humanity's problems, invariably it has been these religions that have *caused* most of them. Oh the havoc comes *not* from the religions per se, but from the weak minded, gullible fools that are *mesmerized* by them . . . and this time I do *not* refer to it as *persuaded!*

Six hundred years before the supposed birth of Jesus conditions in India had become much worse than in Mahatma Gandhi's time, and for the same reasons. The Sudras and out-castes had multiplied into millions and all were living in extreme poverty and ignorance. No group had education, nor decent living facilities except the Brahmins, the highest and ruling caste. All of the other castes had splintered into sub-castes, and when employed at all had the barest of meager living conditions. The pall of being eternally damned to reincarnation and karma finished demoralizing the mobs so that despondency, ill-will, and resentment were resulting in all sorts of trouble and turmoil.

One of the top families of Brahmins, wealthy and aloof to the problems, was King Suddhodhana and Queen Maya who ruled over the Sakyas. This was a tribe of the Gautamas in northern India at the foot of the Himalayas. A son was born to the two rulers in 563 B.C. and they named him Siddhartha Gautama. This boy was raised in the palace, in the lap of luxury, and was given the best of everything, including an education by the top priests and instructors of the highest order.

Siddhartha became as well versed in the Hindu Sacred scriptures and in the scholastic knowledges of the day as anyone in his father's kingdom. When he had completed his education he was given the beautiful Princess Yosodhara to wife, and the two of them, living in the lap of luxury were shielded from all things unpleasant in the world around them. A son was born to them in due course.

This young son had not been in the world very long, when one day Siddhartha went out on a carefree day of fun to hunt game. When returning to his palace with a companion, they came upon a man lying on the ground, writhing in pain. The Prince, protected all his life from knowledge of such things, asked his companion what was wrong with the man. The companion replied: "This is the way of life. All people are liable to become ill and suffer pain." Further along the way, they came upon a very old man, shaky, back bent, and hands atremble, his movements were awkward and uncertain. When the Prince asked what was wrong with the man, his companion explained: "All people grow old and that is the way of old age."

As they continued on their way, the Prince was deeply troubled about the calamity of the sick man, and the trembling, infirm old man. He'd never known such things happened. And then a funeral procession came by. Behind the man being carried to his cremation came his widow and his children, all weeping bitterly. Prince Siddhartha was again perplexed and asked what this sorrowful procession meant.

"That is the way of life. Whether one is a king or a pauper, sooner to some and later to others . . . but death comes to all alike."

These three sights had stunned Siddhartha. Not in his whole life had he ever known about such things. Revelation that life other than the unchanging luxury and total lack of problems he lived in was deeply disturbing. Now, added to that slap in the face was knowledge that he too would age, suffer perhaps painful illness, and eventually die. As he and his companion neared the palace a monk appeared before them with his bowl in his hand, silently begging for his food. The monk's face was calm, untroubled, and serene.

Siddhartha gazed for a long time at the serene face of the monk. As he pondered that serenity, he realized that to meet the challenges of his newly gained information about the human condition, he too needed to "get away from it all" and try to reconcile himself to what he'd learned. He knew he would never achieve that in the company of his family amid the palace splendors and distractions. When he reached the palace, with no explanation or hesitation, he shaved his head, put on the rough garment of a monk, then left with no word to anyone, not even his beautiful young wife. This became known much later to his followers as the "Night of the Great Renunciation."

Seven long years did Siddhartha roam the country side as a homeless, penniless monk, silently begging for food in his bowl as did they. He visited monasteries and learned all he could from other monks, re-studying the sacred Vedas of Hinduism, and the opinions of the monks about them. But nowhere did he find any answers to the deeply troubling questions he wanted answered.

At times he tried asceticism, shunning even the meager sustenance he could get by begging. He often fasted until he fainted, lost weight and health, but his mind worked even less during those periods. He learned the hard way, and finally realized, that self-immolation does NOT lead to wisdom. He began to eat again and slowly regained his health and his mind became clearer.

At long last, when he had diligently tried at length everything he could think of, he sat miserably and tiredly down under a fig tree to meditate. He vowed then and there to not get up nor leave the spot until enlightenment came to him. He stayed there hour after endless hour, rethinking all he knew about the Vedas, what he believed in them and what he rejected. Different accounts describe this length of time in varying ways, but that it was many hours long seems certain. A majority of the accounts say seven long days and nights. The thing that was upper most in Siddhartha's mind was from the Vegas: "From good must come good, and from evil must come evil." It was, he believed, the key to all wisdom. But he realized that idea was nothing new, it being a part of the teaching of Hinduism. It is in fact, the law of Karma. But he began to draw from that some entirely new conclusions. Not only that, but he began to believe that he could now answer his own, or anyone else's disturbing questions about life and the human condition.

At last he sprang up and went quickly to the city of Benares. He gathered about him the monks in that city and preached his first sermon to them. When he'd finished one monk ask him: "Are you a God?"

"No," answered Siddhartha.

"Then are you a Saint?"

"No," was Siddhartha's prompt reply.

"If you are not a God, and not a Saint, then what are you?"

"I am awake," answered the Prince turned beggar.

From that day on, those who became his followers called him Buddha, which in their language simply meant: "One who is awake." (or enlightened.)

Prince Siddhartha Guatama became Buddha when he was about 35 years old. His teachings and following began with that "Sermon at Benares." He was teaching, contrary to the "accepted" Hinduism, that no one had to spend hundreds of lifetimes in endless reincarnations attempting to overcome their karma. Nirvana could be accomplished merely by becoming "enlightened." To those who listened to his teachings, he offered far greater hope than did Hinduism, and more to the point, he too seemed to be renouncing the caste system. No one but the Brahmins could tolerate the condition any way. It was one of the quickest spreading "religious" ideas that ever happened, very quickly flooding across boundaries and into other lands . . . particularly into the orient. To a great extent, the Hindu Yogas (self hypnotizing really) stayed with Buddha's new teachings, as well as some of the Vegas he deemed to be truth. Once again, older religious beliefs and practices, were being incorporated into new ones. Never the less, Buddhism became one of the fastest growing and most widely accepted religions, probably in the history of the world. In India, it almost completely replaced Hinduism for almost than a thousand years.

Then slowly, with great effort by the ruling classes, Hinduism again took control in India. The full return of Hinduism to India, finally accomplished around 500 A.D. brought again all of the adverse conditions described above when it had had full control before. From then until Gandhi's time, India became an ever-worsening pest hole with fully ninety percent of its people living in abject poverty and hopelessness. By that time it was nothing new for the people of *any* Deity type "religious" nation to be subjected to.

What has been portrayed thus far about the formation of Buddhism is generally available in most any city library. Many books giving short histories of world religions are available even to school kids. (And they are mostly ignored by the way.) But of very great significance and almost universally NOT published, is Siddhartha's Prime Path to Nirvana by a total abstinence from ALL sexual activities, thoughts, and practices. As far as I have been able to trace this man's basic fundamentals, he seems to be at least one of the earliest, and probably the first "Holy Man" to consider and teach that sex, ANY sex whatsoever, was a fundamental wrong and the basis of endless Karma and countless reincarnations to overcome it. For those able to wipe sex totally out of mind and practice, beautiful Nirvana was easy to obtain in only one lifetime.

Almost simultaneously, a very powerful king in ancient Persia, Zoroaster, was attacking sexual deeds for another reason entirely. His pet grief was simple and to the point. All nationalities anywhere in Zoroaster's known world at that time openly practiced homosexuality. The King was no fool. He realized that homo acts between men greatly curtailed their screwing women, and THAT cut deeply into the production of new men as taxpayers, soldiers, and the numerical strength of his empire. To make laws against it was futile and he knew it . . . . Ahh! . . . but if homo acts between men became a SIN against the new God being introduced (Mazda), then many men, compelled by their own fear and beliefs in this God, would refrain from or drastically reduce homosexual acts, thus there would be more really productive screwing of women.

Item: Women engaging in lesbianism, did NOT keep them from having children. It did keep them less apt to fuck someone else's husband and therefore cause the loss of another tax-payer due to her enraged husband killing another tax-payer.

Mazda's "Savior Son," Mithra, was born of a virgin earth woman on December 25th. To make fornication an unmistakable "sin," Mithra castrated himself to keep from committing the unpardonable. At the time, thousands of the Israelites were being held as captives by Persia. Up until that time the Israelites had never considered fucking, either with a woman or another man to be sinful. In fact the earlier writings attributed to "Moses" (the first 5 books of The Old Testament) are full of statements, many of them supposedly made by "God" that clearly give permission, and at times even "orders" to fuck someone other than a wife . . . a "handmaiden" (slave) in most cases. (Genesis 16 and 17 are an example of God condoning this out of wedlock fucking.) Godly admonitions against unwed sex did not begin creeping into Jewish writings that would eventually become the Old Testament until AFTER the captive Israelites began being freed from Persia to return to their homeland. The only "Godly" orders against sex until that time had been to prevent a man's "property" (his women) from being reduced in value by screwing away their virginity before being "bought." Now, in the Old Testament, the books Leviticus, Numbers, and Deuteronomy spell out the Zoroaster bans against unwed sex, and male sex with other males in unmistakable detail. The supposed Godly destruction of Sodom and Gomorrah graphically underlines "God's" hatred of homosexuality.

Thus a spoiled rotten brat named Siddhartha not only proved himself to be mentally unstable by his actions, but in that unreliable condition contributed the first fundamental idea that sex was a major cause of displeasing a God and suffering endlessly because of it. Zoroaster, strictly for mercenary reasons adopted similar philosophies which eventually worked their way into Judaism. When we get to the chapters discussing Christianity and its formation we'll portray the total stupidity of the whole war against an intelligent use of our sexuality.

In the meantime there is an interesting side-note to these "Godly" attacks on *natural* sexuality.

The mentally incompetent Siddhartha never recognized women in his philosophies at all. He seemed solely concerned with men and how they could overcome worldly karma. For seven long years after leaving his young wife, there is no record of him ever speaking to or seeking out any woman for any reason. But he spent countless hours conferring and/or listening to other monks, etc. Thus the original Buddhist teachings and their admonitions against sexuality have no mention of women.

Zoroaster on the other hand, saw no harm whatsoever in

women sexually playing with each other. Thus Zoroaster's God Mazda, nor the "Savior Son" Mithra had any orders against lesbianism. So please take note: We often tell you that the entire Judeo-Christian concept is watered-down hash from other religions. Now search the Holy Bible from one end to the other. *You will NOT find one single admonition anywhere in it against lesbianism!* The writers of the Scriptures didn't see any harm in it either. Present day refusal by many different breeds of "Christian" Churches to allow lesbians into their midst is thus clearly seen as a "grafted on" sour branch of their mindless war against sexuality . . . ANY SEXUALITY . . . and NOT something ordered by "God's Word!"

Hinduism returned to full control in India around 500 A.D., mostly by great effort of the Ruling Caste. All the turmoil, crime, birth of bastards, etc. returned. Buddhism went the way of all religions in that it splintered into all sorts of "sects" and "cults." One of the major of these splinters is known as Zen.

CONFUCIANISM:

Religions that have dominated mankind for centuries are divided into three major classifications, which we will get back to presently. One outstanding clue to solving the problems in ANY Society, is to understand that the majority of people raised with-in any one of those major "Religious" communities, invariably become "believers," and thus "slaves" to it. This is unavoidable because they have overwhelming ignorance of the other beliefs. They are taught from birth that theirs is the only *truth*. They also have great ignorance of the *true* history of their own religion's development. However good intentioned or merely self serving it might have been, *ALL* religions, their "accepted" history, and their written material (Torah, Koran, Tao, Old Testament, New Testament, etc., etc.) have been altered, tampered with, deleted from, added to, and generally "improved" until very little credence should remain that any of them were inspired or "protected" by an intelligent God. In any of these religions, alterations to their beliefs, practices, rituals, commandments, "holy" books, etc., has been going on for centuries. It is ignorance of these provable facts that helps enslave millions of people to the religions of their forefathers and their community. The brain-washing begins when the babe is born, and dogs him, warps him, and obfuscates him, throughout his entire life.

America, supposedly the leading, most advanced, and *free* Society in the world, does no better at correcting the above mentioned fallacies then does the poorest, least educated Nation in the world. Unfortunately, to most people, and especially to kids, "history" is a boring and tiresome thing that has all but been eliminated entirely from our "modern" computer addicted school system. "History" isn't even considered important any more. Therefore, as we proceed, I hope my reader will be able to see the handwriting on the wall. Very scant truth is in *any* of the Deity religions or their "sacred" writings. Yet we are on a collision course with disastrous repetition of calamities of the past, for *all* of the great Deity Religions have throughout their entire existence led their followers into utter chaos of needless suffering, deprivation, crime, wars, and mass slaughter.

Confucianism is not a Deity based religion. In simplest definition, it is a philosophy for living. Yet there are vividly apparent parallels in its development to all of the major Deity religions. These, when understood, go a very long ways into showing up the Deity Religions for what they are. If you are a "God" believer, I suggest you fasten your seat belt. Or, if you are determined to live in fear, ignorance, and slavery the rest of your life, you can toss this book in the trash can now.

The same century (600 B.C.) that produced Siddhartha Gautama, also gave birth to Ch'iu K'ung, son of Shu-liang Heih in China. He was not of high princely birth, nor even the son of nobility. By his own words in later life, he repeatedly told his disciples that he was without rank, but from a family of very humble circumstances. Just wait until you see what happened, not only in spite of the records of the day, but also contradictive to his own testimony.

Ch'iu was born in the district of Tsow, province of Lu in 551 B.C. He was the youngest of twelve children. (I hope my reader will have noted that there are a considerable number of authentic records, concerning the birth, parentage, and childhood of kids like Ch'iu and Siddhartha, from over 500 years before the time of Jesus. (In Jerusalem at the time of the supposed birth of Jesus, were many educated writers, and they wrote scads of information about leaders of their day, in records that are still intact. Yet in *none* of these records and writings is *any mention whatsoever* concerning Jesus, his birth, life, death, nor of the many *"miracles"* he is supposed to have done. Not ONE mention is made anywhere, except in what is now called the Bible. Further, we must remind our readers that that "Bible" was not even "created" until the year 375 A.D. Then, it was created by the Greeks. But even the earliest versions of it then, have been lost or purposely destroyed and are no longer available to anyone. How does all of that measure up to the constant insisting our Priests and Preachers do when they repeatedly assure us that God has preserved His *Word* and brought it down to us intact so that we might all be "saved?")

Except for the possibility that Ch'iu might have had one brother, the other of his siblings were not mentioned in the old records, the reason being that they were girls. Girls in the China of then were totally unimportant, mere necessities for men, just as they were considered in the "holy" lands back in Old Testament times with the Jews.

Ch'iu's father died when he was three years old, leaving the family destitute. His mother struggled to support herself and her large family, managing somehow to give her son an education. A good education requires two things: A good teacher, and a good student. Ch'iu, to his mother's great relief, was a brilliant student who absorbed instructions and knowledge as fast as they could be given.

That era in China was a morass of ignorance, poverty, feuding war lords, starvation, pestilence, and disease. In early life, and during all of his studies, this boy constantly tried to conceive of WHY these conditions prevailed, and why something could not be done to ease the burden that hundreds of thousands of his people were laden with. Bright, courageous, and concerned, he was already dreaming and scheming of ways that might be accomplished. Considering the plight of the hordes of oppressed people, his meditations blamed the War Lord Feudal system of the day. He realized that an entirely different, peaceful, and helpful Governmental system needed to replace the one they suffered under. But his rebellious side was counter-balanced by his desire to create a method of living and thinking, a *belief*, that would guarantee for its practitioner, peace and well being under *any* problem or condition at all.

That, is a whale of an order.

As with all concepts of forming a "religion" that has ever succeeded, Ch'iu borrowed from beliefs and practices that were already followed by his people. Determined to find an idea that would promote a peaceful and honest government, he realized that a prime necessity for it, would be one that would *educate* the ignorant masses, and at the same time teach and train them in skills by which they could make a decent living. Consider all of that very carefully, for in truth, our own government here, has never yet accomplished any of it. Far worse, we've let stupid judges, bribed lawmakers, self-serving and powerful unions, the whole bunch all too well laced with bigotry and incompetent management, succeed in turning our schooling system into a dung heap of failure. Over half of our adult population is functionally illiterate, many thousands of them graduates of our high schools. They know very little about their government and how it is supposed to work, even less about history.

Even while still a child, Ch'iu loved everything ancient and traditional. The Chinese have always honored their elderly and their ancestors. Taught these traditions from birth on, and being fully convinced of their importance, it was only natural that they became also a part of his budding philosophies.

Ch'iu married at age 18, and soon his dwelling became a

meeting place for neighbors who sought his advice and counseling. He had a great capacity for understanding and appreciating the problems of others. But he also was gifted with a remarkable ability to influence and teach those who came to listen. Brilliant and studious all of his life, nowhere else could the people find anyone as well versed in history and tradition of the ancients as he was. As we've already shown, his full name was Ch'iu K'ung. Those he taught and impressed, soon began referring to him as K'ung fu tse, which translated means Kung the philosopher. There was absolutely *nothing* militant in K'ung's teaching, nor in his manner and practices. This should give you some idea of just how ridiculous are the movies, TV series, and beliefs in our own country today about Kung Fu. In the first place it is a chopped off title which obliterates its actual meaning. Thus all that we have come to believe, watch, practice, and accept about Kung Fu is not only patently ridiculous, but it is also a total lie.

In his early twenties, K'ung quit his meager paying job and devoted full time to studying, teaching and counseling. His audiences and pupils multiplied as his fame spread and he was able to make a living from the fees and gifts. His fame as a teacher spread throughout his Province of Lu. He also had many students who could not afford to pay him anything whatsoever. He never refused to give them as much of his time and attention as he did to those who could pay. It was a part of his beliefs. This increased his fame and popularity as people began to see that he practiced what he taught.

K'ung had many philosophies which would serve and help us today fully as much as they helped the people of his Province in his day. When a pupil showed no interest at all in what K'ung was teaching, he would single that person out for a personal consultation. During that session K'ung would do everything possible to get the student to open up and state his own views, beliefs, or lack of them . . . to question, argue, or disagree . . . to display any interest at all. He not only had great ability to teach, but a definite talent for opening a person up. If his great talents could not open that student up, get him to expressing opinions nor questioning, K'ung would never bother seeing or trying to teach that person again. When asked why, he replied:

> "To *not* teach a capable person is to waste that man. To try to teach an incapable person is to waste a teacher." Through countless writings, speeches, and sayings, it becomes more than apparent that K'ung had no time or patience whatsoever for stupidity, and a person from whom he, with his great ability, could not get a rise out of, was hopelessly stupid. His own words were: "If he has no interest what ever in learning, and none can be awakened in him, then he is hopelessly stupid."

Today, American tax-payers are docilely watching tens of billions of dollars of their money being squandered trying to teach many thousands of students who do not have and will never acquire, the ability to learn what is being taught. Sadly it is wasting not only money and teacher time. The greatest waste of all is the time and ability of the students who can, and *would* learn much, much more if they were not totally hamstrung and held back in classes wasting time with the dullards who can't learn nor keep up. Teachers are forced to slow down and repeat and explain and re-explain in a vain effort to try to teach grossly stupid students. They are quite plentiful and haphazardly mixed into our school room classes like so much sand mixed into the sugar bowl . . . and with just about the same results. K'ung knew instinctively that bending to try to raise the stupid ones amongst us up to our own level, succeeds only in lowering our own position down to conform more nearly with theirs. It *never* raises the dullards any higher. Why America has not already learned this, and apparently cannot learn it, is beyond comprehension.

So great did K'ung's fame become that people of his city came to him, asked him to become Chief Magistrate of their town. Crimes of all sorts and kinds were epidemic over the whole Province of Lu and the prisons were bulging full. K'ung accepted the invitation, eager to prove that his teachings would work. After only one year in office he had introduced so many reforms and new ways of doing things, that the city had become crime free and word of this had spread throughout the whole Province of Lu. All of it came to the attention of the Governor of Lu, and that man came to seek audience with K'ung.

When questioned, K'ung had this to say: "To govern simply by statute and to maintain order by means of penalties, is to render the people secretive, evasive, and devoid of a sense of shame." He also went to great length to explain that there could not be a successful government that had two different levels of enforcement, one for the destitute and overworked peasants, and another for the high ones in command of government. The lower classes were punished with extreme harshness, even cruelty, while those in power bribed and/or overlooked nefarious deeds in their own circle. "If all don't observe the same rules and mete the same justice, then none shall."

The Governor appointed K'ung to be the Minister of Justice for the entire Province of Lu. Again K'ung's methods worked and in very short time, crime had evaporated and the prisons were empty. High ranking officials of other Provinces became disturbed. If K'ung's success attracted the Emperor of China, their own nefarious and lucrative manipulations could be lopped off. A group of them got their heads together and pulled off a big enough bribe to again corrupt the Governor of Lu and some of his top officials. K'ung was ousted, his methods discarded. Very quickly a disgruntled populace became again infested with criminal activities and the prisons filled to overflowing again.

Broken hearted, K'ung spent several years working in various provinces, trying to convince each Governor, get them to try his methods. He always wondered why he could get no other Governor to even try. He spent the last few years of his life compiling his great ideas into written form.

Westerners cannot pronounce K'ung Fu Tse as it is pronounced in Chinese. The nearest we can come to it, is Confucius.

For all practical purposes, with the death of K'ung, his followers quickly forgot his teachings and returned to the sorrowful state of times before he began trying to teach them. Please pay particular attention to that. In a moment you shall see why K'ung's workable ideas were forgotten when he no was no longer there to keep pushing them.

K'ung died at age 72. For awhile his most ardent followers gathered together and began assembling every written thing of his they could find. His Doctrines of the Middle Path were one of the series they preserved. They did NOT consider his works to be a Religion! To them he was a Great Teacher, an educator and statesman, with no "holy" attributes at all. But this idea was held only by his closest disciples. During the years he wandered from Province to Province trying to teach and attract some Governor to his reform ideas, there occurred a movement which is the primary reason I've included Confucianism in this book. People who had heard his great speeches began to talk of him to others who had not yet heard him.

Human nature has never changed. People try to impress other people. In this attempt, they have seemly a built-in need to elaborate . . . make what they say the more convincing. So not only did people who'd heard K'ung speak try to repeat some of the great man's words and ideas, but their elaboration turned into *exaggeration*. Tales of all sorts began to circulate about K'ung's "magical" powers and this quickly was embellished with wondrous things that happened on earth when he was born: "There was a "super" brilliant star in the east to announce his arrival when he was born." "In far away lands, idols and their temples crumbled and fell when he was born." "On the night he was born many long dead ancestors appeared to their families to announce the glad tidings."

These exaggerations became wilder and even more embellished. "He cured a cripple who'd been unable to walk since birth. And he cured him simply by placing his hands on the man's useless legs." "He restored the eyes of a man who was blinded years ago in an accident."

Eventually K'ung learned of these sayings. He was furious. Openly and publicly before huge audiences he denounced and put the lie to all these rumors of his miraculous powers, and told the truth of his humble birth and raising by a destitute widow with her huge brood. The results? The tales got even worse, adding all sorts of "Miraculous" powers and events to K'ung's credit. Since he'd never asked to be credited with anything, desired only to teach and to help sadly deprived throngs, his message was forgotten when he moved on to other locales. There'd been no "hocus-pocus" or Godly mysticism to keep it alive. When he died, only his very closest followers began trying to preserve his ideas and teachings.

I hope you've not missed one of the main points of this story. Those tales of K'ung's miraculous birth signs and abilities were being circulated, yes and *written* about in documents that are still available, *over 500 years before a very similar birth is said to have occurred in Bethlehem! This "alleged" birth in Bethlehem was NOT written about until nearly a century after it was claimed to have happened!*

But don't panic yet. This is just one small genie risen from our bottle. As we continue, each new genie rising from it, will be more startling . . . and more formidable.

A hundred years after the death of K'ung, another "special" child was born in Lu, the same province as he had been. Early on the mother became disturbed as she noticed her son doing very credible mimicking of other people he saw. She did NOT want him copying after the people in her locale, for they were an undesirable kind, so she moved her family to other places. In each she found him again doing remarkably accurate parodies of those he saw. Again and again she moved until at last she settled in a center of education and teachers. In no time at all her boy was duplicating the politeness, and studious nature of the center's teachers. There she was pleased to remain.

The boy's name was Mang. Mimicking the teachers soon attracted him to actually *doing* what they did . . . studying and trying to learn. He quickly became an avid and brilliant scholar. Through his research and study at the center, he found the preserved works of K'ung. It was as if he'd found a rare treasure. Immediately he was convinced about the truth and worth of K'ung's philosophies. He not only began an in depth study of all the works, he began writing, compiling, and preserving his own thoughts and opinions about them. He organized the writings of K'ung into books, the best known of which is *THE BOOK OF ANALECTS*. He also began to gather other students, and even teachers about him, to lecture them on the philosophies of K'ung. In a very short while he became known to his listeners as Mang tze (Mang the philosopher). From that beginning we get the name Mencius.

Mencius had great talent and ability. Where-ever he spoke he gathered converts to his way of thinking, and it was not long until his listeners began attaching a "religious" reverence to him and his teachings. K'ung began to be thought of as the teacher of a new religion, and by association, K'ung Fu tse became the "holy" man who had brought the religion to earth.

It is another important milestone to understanding Religions, to consider the Six major principles of K'ung Fu tze.

1. Human nature is good; and evil is essentially unnatural.

2. Man is free to conduct himself as he will, and he is the master of his choice.

3. Virtue is its own reward. If one does good for a reward, or avoids evil for fear of punishment . . . that is not virtue.

4. What you do not want others to do to you, do not do to them.

5. A man has five duties: To his ruler, to his father, to his wife (and she to him); to his elder brother, to his friend, The most important of these is the filial duty.

6. Man should strive to become a superior man.

Now hold the phone. Particularly look at number 4. K'ung Fu tze conceived and wrote these principles some 500 years before the time of Jesus. Mang tze was compiling and teaching them nearly 400 years before Jesus. The "Holy" Bible quoting Jesus as saying the same thing, was not compiled and created until 375 years after the death of Jesus . . . .

. . . . oh there is more, much more. But don't let it worry you . . . . yet. Hopefully, by the end of this book you will have begun to understand number 1. above, why it seems to be false, and have a desire to fulfill number 6.

Due to Mang's considerable ability as a proselytizer, teacher, and organizer, soon there were dozens of large groups over a very wide area in China, busily engaged in hearing and studying K'ung's principles for living. In communities where large groups formed, much of the stress of crime, poverty, and ignorance began slowly to be lessened. This led to their reserving small areas to meditate upon the principles responsible for the improvements in their lives. This of course led to the building of small shrines in these areas, and later still to the building of Pagodas where-in the "faithful" could meditate and "communicate" with the "Spirit" of their newly found mentor. Without his ever being aware of it, K'ung had begun a much revered and believed in . . . Religion!

Like every other religion ever conceived, it has splintered into dozens of diversified "cults" and practices, one group stressing one thing, another off on an entirely different set of ritualistic absurdities.

Psychiatrists and researchers into the human condition, long ago began to know that man makes fun of, in supposed to be joke form, those things he is uneasy about, or fears. Few people are aware of that. Even fewer have attached any importance to the fact that "types" of jokes are a "fad" thing. They are told, as a "type," in mass profusion for a while, then die out to be replaced by another "type" that enjoys wide popularity for its period. Well before World War II, just to name a few of the passing "fads," were the "Pat and

Mike" stories. For awhile, everywhere you went, everyone you talked to, had a "new" Pat and Mike story to tell. Then came the tidal wave of "Absent Minded Professor stories." ("Hey! Did you hear about the absent minded Professor? He was so absent minded that he kissed the street car goodbye and rode his wife to town.") In the mid-30's came the deluge of "Confucius Says" quotes, all of them making fun of the Confucianism teachings. Nearly all of K'ung Fu tse's teachings were in the form of short quotes. His follower's would thus teach by saying: "K'ung Fu tse says that . . . . etc. etc." So here in America the rash broke out in this manner: "Confucius Says: Secretary not permanent fixture 'til screwed on desk." or "Confucius Says: Aviatrix who fly plane upside down have crack up."

Just before WW II got us into it, the "Little Moron" stories were hot. Tons and tons of war material were vital and our factories were humming 24 hours a day. But management discovered that countless hours of worker's time was being squandered by the little moron stories. Workers at all levels just had to tell each other the "latest" one, and of course the listener would have to respond with his "latest" one. It would be just seconds before a group had formed, ignoring their work, and the tales would be one right after the other. Management, the Government, and even the FBI, became highly involved trying to stop the stories. Effective? Not really. Little Moron had about run his course anyway and was replaced by the Tojo and Hitler stories. Employees everywhere, with a hot new passion, wasted even more time on those. When Poland was over-run and gruesome accounts of the happenings there permeated our news reports, the "dumb Pollack" stories filled our ears on all sides. It was America's "protective" reaction from the real stories of atrocities being committed against the hapless Poles.

During the days of the "Freedom Riders" and the gut wrenching mistreatment they and Negroes were dealt with by prejudiced and bigoted nincompoopery, the "nigger" stories became thicker than the fog in London on a dreary winter morn. Stories about the two most involved Governors in the fight were also rife. As an eternally convenient stand-by, the Priest and Preacher stories of misdeeds, particularly sexual misdeeds, are always eagerly listened to.

All of the above is only scratching the surface of human confusion about things they are uneasy about or fearful of. But to thoroughly understand our joke telling and willingness to listen, we must now recognize one ever present fact in at least 90 per cent of the jokes. Sex, and/or bodily functions, have always predominated all and every one of the type "fads" we've become hooked on. Thus it is easy for a thinking person to see, that sex, nudity, and bodily functions are our most aggravating uncertainty. Mentally and morally, most American's past the age of 12, become morbidly obsessed with sexual needs, problems, and questions they *cannot* resolve. Practices, desires, and realistic knowledge concerning sex have been too hideously maimed. As the twig is bent, so grows the tree.

But for the moment, let us not seek a solution. Let us first become more fully acquainted with the problem.

All of the major religions throughout the past 3,000 years have followed almost identical formats. Most of them were created by people so uninformed that they thought the world was flat. If you ventured too far, you'd fall off. They knew nothing of the wide variety of people on other continents and islands. With Gautama, K'ung, and Mang, their motives were altruistic. Each tried to ease suffering, poverty, and ignorance of their fellow men. None of their philosophies had any militant, nor subversive aims in conception nor practice. They were not designed nor intended to control, but to assist and elevate those who had mind enough to try. The "philosophy" forming those movements was turned into "religions" by those who followed, not by the founders. There were no "Commandments" of a "God" to compel anyone to do anything. Thus, spread of the Religions has always been peaceful and persuasive, an attraction to think, NOT by the use of force.

The second type of Religion, those with a supposed "God" dictating them, were invariably militant, brutal, and aggressive.

Basically they were designed to *control* people, not to help them. Also, each of them were aimed specifically at *replacing* an existing Religion that was hampering what the founders of the new ones wanted to achieve. But here again is that tiresome old demon, history. Let's examine a bit more of that before we form opinions of who or what is really in charge of our "souls." After all, if most of us are doomed to spend an eternity writhing in an unbearably cruel Hell, we at least should understand why.

I've shown examples of how religions were created and changed as new generations took over. Some of you may have raised skeptical eyebrows as to how that pertains to *your* particular belief. Let's look at a Religion that demonstrates "tampering" fully. It is the best way to demonstrate an indisputable fact.

CHAPTER FOUR

TAOISM:

Until more facts may be unearthed by research, the origins of Hinduism are clouded indeed. Also very obscure are the beginnings of Mazda and his savior son Mithra. Some of the once powerful long ago old religions became so obscure that we cannot even find a name for them. But for one man, who is recorded in history, and even had audience at least once with K'ung Fu Tze, we know almost nothing of his name, origin, or death. But we do know that he was indeed strange.

His name is nowhere recorded that I have ever been able to find. His acquaintances knew him as Lao Tze, which means The Old Philosopher. No one knew where he came from, or anything of his parentage. Even so, he had managed to acquire a considerable number of disciples and followers at the same time K'ung Fu Tze was becoming famous himself. Since these two worked in the same locale, K'ung's followers began telling him of a strange old man who spoke of a far-out metaphysical doctrine. K'ung, all of his life disturbed by the unusual, the enigmatic, and the inscrutable, arranged to have a meeting with the man. He had no intentions whatsoever of arguing or disagreeing. It was his sole purpose to learn what the other thought, or gain new insights from him. He wanted to compare their different philosophies.

The meeting was a disaster from the beginning.

K'ung was very deeply into tradition, respect for others, and manners. Following the tradition of respect when meeting formally with another for the first time, K'ung bedecked himself in his finest formal attire. In Chinese tradition this indicated he had very high regard for the person he was having audience with.

Lao tze was not only unimpressed, he was pointedly contemptuous. He criticized not only K'ung's attire, which he deemed to be putting on vain "airs," but also the reverence and importance K'ung practiced and taught toward dead ancestors. "Those of whom you teach are naught but ashes in their graves." (impatiently) Kung tried to explain his belief that new knowledge must be based upon old knowledge. "Put away your polite airs and your vain display of fine robes. A wise man does not display his treasure to those he does not know . . . nor can he learn justice from the ancients." "Why not?" asked K'ung.

"It is not bathing that makes the pigeon white," said Lao tze contemptuously, and abruptly stalked out, breaking off the interview before it had gotten anywhere.

James Legge, famed British translator of the monumental *Chinese Classics*, when writing of this meeting, stated that neither of the two men ever touched on the comparative antiquity of *both* their views. I fully concur with that opinion, not just between these two ancient sages, but as to the identical problem existing in the teachings of ALL religions. Coinciding with, and exactly duplicating it, the evolution of human kind has led to an identical evolution of his "Gods" and his religions. Each and every religion that exists on this earth today, and all those hundreds of long forgotten religions of the past, have *never* been anything more than cold and stale left-overs from superstitiously formed beliefs before them. The reason I decided to include Taoism in this book is because it and its history so thoroughly demonstrate that evolutionary phenomena. Once that is seen and understood, then the observer can begin recognizing identical absurdity in ALL religions.

Interpreting all that can be learned from historical records, Lao tze was about 50 years older than K'ung, which made him somewhere in the mid-seventies at the time of his meeting with K'ung. Lao was an archivist at the Imperial Library and it was through his curt, puzzling, and disturbing statements to those he dealt with that his renown as a very wise sage was shaped. It was from this rapidly spreading fame, that K'ung heard of him. As near as can be determined, Lao never formally addressed any group for any reason, did not try to teach any one anything, and did not seek disciples nor followers. Yet over many years he apparently accumulated a very impressive and wide spread multitude of people who believed him to be more than merely mortal.

After many years at the library, when Lao was in his nineties, he quit the job determined to leave that area because he disapproved of the rulers and their heavy handed authority. He bought a small cart and a black ox, loaded his belongings and headed for the border. At the border outpost a guard, a man named Yin Hai, recognized and stopped him.

"NO!" said Yin Hai. "You've always kept to yourself like a hermit and have never written any of the things you know and teach. Yet many have learned from you. Now you want to leave and your teachings will die with you. I will NOT let you cross the border until you have written down the essentials of your teachings."

So Lao tze, as quickly as possible, did as he was told. He wrote five thousand Chinese characters, a work he divided into eighty-one short poems, and called it Tao Teh King. He handed it to the guard. "This is all I have to teach. Now let me pass."

"Not until I have checked."

It was a small booklet of only about 25 pages, and did not take Yin Hai long to read it. When he'd finished, he laid it reverently on his guard post table, turned and begged Lao tze to let him go too, be a servant and disciple. Lao agreed. Yin crawled up on to the cart and the two crossed the border . . . never to be heard of again, nor to cause any more notices in any records that have ever been found.

The book was something else. It was found and turned over to the authorities. Over the centuries it has been the cause for many highly educated and informed people to write a very impressive number of huge, thick tomes, all trying to explain Tao Teh King's meaning. For example, there are many diverse opinions as to what the word Tao means. There are disagreements as to whether it was *Tao Teh King or Tao Teh Ching*. There are differences in the meaning as well as in the pronunciation. Many think that Tao means the "way," and many say the "path." But a very large group of equally accredited scholars believe that Tao means the "The Word," in the same sense as the Apostle John used it in the New Testament. Earlier heavy, thick books trying to explain the simple little 25 pager, gave rise to secondary view points which resulted in still more thick "explanatorily" tomes, essays, papers, and so on. One can now find and read so many various opinions by so many supposedly competent researchers, that by the time you've waded through a dozen or so, you'll be more mystified than when you first heard of the subject.

But that is only the beginning. The tens of thousands of people who, over the centuries have become followers of Tao, have been, and still are, the personification of, and the exact template of ALL religious believers, through-out human history. First, Lao Tze *never*, in the little book or by word of mouth, expressed any "Religious" convictions or desire to create any. Yet many people who have read his works, both in original reprint versions, and in the scholarly "explanations," have seen in the writings a very definite teaching of a Supreme Being, referred to by some as the First Cause. These types of opinions caused those sharing them to band together and begin turning *Tao Teh Ching* into a Religion, together with "Shrines," icons, and temples. Rituals, homilies, oms, and prayers soon became the main body of belief. From this, again as always has happened with ANY religious movement, the big groups began to splinter into various sects and cults, no small portion of them gradually reverting to Pagan worship of Nature. In our just ended century, games, methods of forecasting one's fortune, all sorts of Pop Art, Pop Psychology, etc., were developed, which had nothing whatsoever to do with Lao Tze's little book or its meanings, *but are directly derived from some of the beliefs it gave birth to!*

No matter which belief about Tao is being followed by anyone professing it, arguing or trying to point out errors in thinking about it, is as pointless and useless as arguing with a Christian about Jesus, or arguing with a stump . . . which incidentally, displays about the same amount of reasoning ability as anyone brain-washed with a religion.

One interesting side note: Many years before I began researching Tao and its history, as part of an assignment while I was a student in a large and well endowed University, I had to read and report on a certain sonnet. It was hailed by the Professor of Literature who lectured our class, as one of the finest sonnets ever written. To avoid possible legal problems, I will not name the sonnet or its author. Okay, so I got through the semester and even made a reasonably decent grade. But that sonnet stuck with me, because it was perhaps the most disturbing one I ever read. It caused a whole new way to think about many things. It was written by a man watching a horse drawn carriage that was transporting a man to his grave.

And lo, nearly fifty years after reading that sonnet, in preparation for this chapter, I read some of *Tao Teh Ching*. I got knocked clear off my pins when reading Chapter XI of the little 25 page book. It is titled THE THIRTY SPOKES.

"The thirty spokes unite in the one nave; but it is on the empty space for the axle, that the use of the wheel depends. Clay is fashioned into vessels; but it is on their empty hollowness, that their use depends. The door and windows are cut out from the walls to form an apartment; but it is on the empty space within, that its use depends. Therefore, what has a positive existence serves for profitable adaptation, and what has not that for actual usefulness."

Approximately twenty-five hundred years after Lao Tze wrote that in his strange little book for the guard, another man plagiarized that first sentence and its meaning to write one of the most disturbing sonnets I ever read . . . and all he or Lao either was showing is how thoroughly we put stress and importance on the wrong things.

I believe, again very disturbingly, that the whole human race has put stress and importance on the wrong things for their entire history on earth . . . all without ever realizing, pursuing, nor practicing the *vital and important things!* Just as the thirty spokes are nothing, and useless, if the empty hole in the nave is missing, so are all of our religions beliefs when they continually promote havoc and suffering rather than peace and well being.

Y'Ching anyone? Perhaps you even have a set in your home. So now you know where it came from. You can also now know that it, like the spokes on the wheel, has no use, except to hold up the empty hole in the head of people who think mystic or "spiritual" Beings influence and control our existence.

Any in depth study of the ancient beliefs and how they became "religions" when multitudes began trying to understand and practice them, soon reveals to the seeker that each is but a parody of the others. In any and all of these developments, as millions of people were mesmerized into "believing" the particular credo they were subjected to, their attempted "faith" practices became saturated and obsessed with "rituals" and chants, rather than reasoning and sanity.

Few indeed are the humans who are not stirred by a rhythmic beat . . . a "pulse" might we say? Do you not know that ALL of the bipeds, whether monkey, ape, or orang, are similarly affected? And has it not been proved that repetition, especially that delivered in pulsing "beat" is hypnotic? Now go to church next Sunday morn and learn. First, observe the "atmosphere" of the church and its interior. Whether the congregation gathers for a funeral, wedding, christening, baptism, or regular worship, the nave of that church is full of doom, gloom, and pessimism. All there must repent living and be saved, for in that nave, inevitable death stares each and all continually in the face. The music, a rhythmic "pulse," lulls senses and reasoning. Has anyone ever heard a NEW sermon there? NO. That too is monotony and repetition, identical to all others intoned in similar naves for two thousand years. Read an authoritative book of instructions on hypnotism and you will begin to understand.

So I'll give you a mini-sermon the Priests and Preachers never will. In all of provable history, Nature has *never* heeded *any* of the Commandments of ANY God! I deem this *not* the unruly nor blasphemous proclivities of Nature. But certainly it *must be that, or a non-existence of God!*

CHAPTER FIVE

Opposites are how we know what neither is.

It is indicative of problems when comparing religions to note that those developed centuries ago in the Far East were philosophical, conceived in sane thinking to ease suffering of countless, hapless, oppressed people. None of them concentrated on controlling people, but rather to free them from oppression, ignorance, and poverty. No other motive of the originators can be found except their concern and altruism.

But oh how different are the Deity Religions! Not one of them concerned itself with human welfare, or well being, while the person was alive! Every facet of each of them was concerned primarily with an "alleged" *soul* of humans after they were dead. Yet the smartest and sharpest humans that have ever lived have *never* produced any reasonable evidence whatsoever that a "soul" exists. The "soul" is a pipe dream of extremely ancient people who also believed that every thing in Nature was an individual Spirit, manifesting itself into solid forms that humans could see. Refining, improving, or up-dating fantasy pipedreams has never yet produced a reality.

In the far East, altruistic philosophies for a better way of life were turned into "religions" by those who needed a crutch to lean on. Life, for them, is too much without it. But in areas surrounding the Mediterranean Sea, "Gods" were invented as a powerful tool to form religions that *subjected and controlled* people.

These opposites are how we know what neither is!

Today in America, attacking or decrying Christian beliefs is similar to swimming nude from Honolulu to San Francisco, with a boat a few hundred feet in front of you tossing out shark attractive morsels. With-in our Christian multitudes however, a certain uneasiness is being felt because of the extremely rapid growth and acceptance of Islam. Small wonder! Even most of these people do not realize that mega-movement successes like the "Promise Keepers," (and there are others) are nothing but Islam's subversive infiltrations. In spite of all God, Jesus, our Priests, Preachers, and law-makers can do, Islam is the fastest growing religion on this world, and also in America. This unstoppable phenomena should be closely examined to determine its merits . . . . and also its asininity.

It is not generally well known, but to find the roots of Islam we must first consult our own Holy Bible. So for the moment, let us have a Bible Study Hour. That should please (and hopefully placate) many Christians.

In the book of Genesis, Abram (later named Abraham by God), and his wife Sarah, have no children because Sarah has never conceived. The aging Sarah, knowing that this is contrary to what God has promised Abraham, that great nations will come from his loins, tells him to take her hand-maiden Hagar to bed. (In the Bible, in that long ago day, a hand-maiden was a slave. Thus *any* order given to her, HAD to be obeyed.) So Abraham took Hagar for a roll in the hay and Hagar conceived. Just as God had promised, Abraham had a son, whom he named Ishmael. All of this happened as God was getting ready to destroy Sodom and Gomorrah, but that is another story for another time.

Many years later, when both Abraham and Sarah are well into their 90's, God again derails nature and causes the aging, infirm, and life long inability of Sarah to conceive, to be altered. She conceives and bears him another son, which he names Isaac. Then, as all good stories must show, the plot thickens. Practices and beliefs of the era were that the first son inherited the father's estate, and the holdings of Abraham were considerable. Abraham's legitimate heir therefore was Ishmael, son of a slave, while Isaac, his son by Sarah, would get nothing. Sarah was greatly disturbed, centuries of time, nor her age, seemingly ever changing a woman's way of harassing a husband. She demanded of Abraham that he get rid of the two. Wifely anger and demands usually give a husband great trouble and this was no exception. Abraham loved his son by Hagar. Keep in mind that Isaac was just at weaning age, and Ishmael was still a small boy. Today we have much heavy handed action by Churches, Government, and all sorts of "do-gooders" to force men to take responsibility for kids that result from a bit of fun they have poked at a woman.

Maybe all these "do-gooders" haven't read the Bible. In that long ago day, when God was dealing directly with Abraham, He sided with Sarah and bade the man to kick Hagar and Ishmael out. However, kicking them out in that area, and in that era, was considerably different from here and now. No settlement of any kind could long survive in that area without water, for all the whole countryside is raw burning desert, usually with many scorching hot miles between places where water could be obtained. So early the following morning, Abraham rose, gave Hagar a small bottle of water and a bit of bread. Then he had her and Ishmael removed from his abode and marooned out on the burning sands of an endless desert. Our Bible says that God "opened" Sarah's eyes so that she could see a well of water, thus letting her and the boy survive. No mention is made of food, but anyway, Ishmael grows up to be an archer.

All of that was a folklore story told by the "Children of Israel" for many centuries before it was finally written as they developed their first crude form of writing. The writing was Aramic, gradually learned by Israelites about 750 B.C. In the meantime, folklore legends usually spread, and in the days when these stories were being born and circulated, they invariably became accepted by more than one tribe or locale and frequently more than one race of people. The story of Abraham was one of the oldest and apparently very popular with all who heard it, and so, let us look at another version of it.

Across endless wastes of desert from where the "Children of Israel" were telling the story, another race was enjoying the same yarn, but with notable differences. Except for Yahweh's part in it, the two different versions are about the same up until the time that Abraham has Hagar and Ishmael hauled out into the desert and abandoned. There the two versions, one no less ridiculous than the other, part company.

In this episode, Hagar has again put her small son down and gone a few steps away to sit down and die. In both this version, and our Bible's, she went a small ways apart from him so she wouldn't have to watch him die. When he sees his mother suffering, he rises, walks over to her and kicks the sand with his heel. Immediately a bubbling fresh spring bursts forth out of the hot sand. So Hagar and Ishmael abide by the spring. Soon a caravan comes along and its members are astonished to see a new bubbling spring of fresh water where none has ever been before. After replenishing their own water bags, they hasten on to find Abraham, who with his wealth of possessions is a great leader in his area. When he hears their report he is naturally astonished and dashes out to see the miracle for himself.

Anyone who has ever ventured very far on a desert can imagine old Abraham's reaction when he saw the fresh bubbling spring. He named it Zemzem (the spring of Ishmael) and near it he built the Kaaba (the cube). In the Kaaba, he placed the Black Stone, which had been handed down to him as an inheritance from Adam. Adam stole the Black Stone from the Garden of Eden when he and Eve were kicked out. God's security wasn't very good at the Garden of Eden. Worse still, his press agents were loafing, for while the "story" spread over into another race, "God" as the one they should worship, hadn't been heard of. Tch, tch.

Many people began to come to drink the magic "healing" waters of Zemzem, to kiss the Black Stone, to meditate in the Kaaba. "Gods" (plural) were responsible for the miracle. Names were given to them. Artisans made idols to represent the gods. Some were placed in the Kaaba; some mounted in niches outside and around the shrine.

When opportunity knocks, some folks hear and cash in. People who came to meditate and drink had to cross many miles of burning desert to get there. By the time they reached the Kaaba they were low on food and water. Camel traders were quick to see the need, and to bring camel caravans with food and other useful items to sell. Shaded areas were furnished by the caravan's tents; these gave way to buildings. First a town, then a city rose around the Kaaba. It was named Mecca. Mecca became a "holy" city, and with its gods legion already, they quickly began to multiply.

Opportunists saw gods in practically everything in nature, and of course a god required an idol to represent himself to the worshipping masses. Any tree, rock, mountain, or animal might "reveal" its "real" god self to the wise with the eye to see, and soon there were literally hundreds of idols representing the various "gods" so discovered. Fortunes in tributes became standard fare for those who had been smart enough to hear opportunity knocking . . . and the hundreds making pilgrimages to Mecca soon became confused and diverse in their various worshipping practices of the many God-Idols. "Cults" of varied rituals and beliefs sprang up everywhere, some putting more importance on one group of gods, others catering to a different set of the many gods available. Merchants in Mecca, already making fortunes from the swarms of people who made pilgrimages there, began to visualize another gold mine. Why should the magic waters of Zemzem be free?

If we remember that most all of Arabia is desert, that the tens of thousands of inhabitants lived in far flung tribes clustered around spots where water was available, that to make the pilgrimage to Mecca was a "must do" but arduous trek of many days, then we can see the picture more clearly. Zem zem was blocked off and the water was no longer free, but sold. It did not matter whether the water was magic or not. Any caravan that came to Mecca was almost out of water by the time it got there. Not only would they need water for themselves and their animals while there to worship, but their water bags would all have to be filled completely to make the long journey back home. The rich merchants got richer, and the "faithful worshippers" continued to be bled, for all they were worth.

It has never mattered about the race, the locale, the government, or the god. Identical conditions have always, throughout all provable history, been the same. Please don't forget that identical conditions, always lead to identical results.

The people began to be despondent, grossly unhappy, and unfulfilled. Street fights, crime, wife stealing, theft of merchandise and water, murder and mayhem became common. Fortunetellers, magic elixirs, diviners of all sorts and kinds sprang up everywhere, for the Gods, even though lavishly funded by the faithful were not answering any prayers.

But for the moment let's back off and take a look at the whole picture. That may be the *only* real hope for the human race. I believe that the greatest problem Americans have today, is NOT understanding what the problem is!

When their religion had become so oppressive in India that its masses were in a cauldron of despondency, lethargy, crime, and unhappiness, Siddhartha Gautama became Buddha by telling the people what they wanted to hear, that they did NOT have to serve out their karma in endless lifetimes forever. When the millions of people in China were at their lowest under the feudalistic regimes they suffered from, K'ung Fu tze created the beginnings of a gargantuan religion by telling them what they wanted to hear, that there was a way to escape their plight and live in peace and harmony.

In 1930, '31, and '32, during one of the worst worldwide depressions in history, Germany had become a seething quagmire of despondency, malcontent and poverty. An obscure, unknown little pip-squeak there, rose to become one of the most powerful and destructive Dictators in modern history, by telling the people what they wanted to hear . . . that the world, and the Jews particularly, had fucked the Germans out of what was rightfully theirs. He cinched this even further, by telling them that their race was the superior race and by "God Given *Rights*," they were entitled to take back what was theirs! From all that developed on account of him, he was almost single-handedly responsible for the unnecessary slaughter of nearly ten million people, many thousands of them little kids. And today, despite all evidence to the contrary, thousands of little groups all over the world, still admire the man's stinking philosophy and think he was right.

In a long endured era in Russia, while under the Totalitarian heel of the Tsars, the populace became a living morass of poverty, despondency, and dissatisfaction. Catholicism was their dominant religion but in no way effective in bringing any solace to any of the mobs of "poor" people, which included every inhabitant except the Tsars, their nobility, and their immediate families. This small group lived in the lap of luxury, while the people had nothing. But one man told them what they wanted to hear . . . that all the goodies and wealth of the world was rightfully theirs . . . . all they had to do was take it. Listening to that "ism," thousands of peasants swarmed into the domain of the Tsar's, butchered the nobility, male and female, then set up the "People's" Government, right according to the dream that the fruitcake had sold them on. It became known as Communism. There was never, in the long history of Communism, any real victory. The oppressed people under the Tsars merely got a new boss; their unpaid for labors never ceased, nor were they eased. If anything, their poverty only became slightly less, in that they now had "pie in the sky" to dream about. The pie never materialized because Lenin, Marx, nor any of the rabble-rousers that led Nations like the Kremlin had ever known how to bake one. The Communistic Idea (pipe dream) had already failed miserably, two thousand years before Lenin was born. Nevertheless, millions of believers in it gave enough power to their new leaders, that they came perilously close to launching a nuclear holocaust that would have wiped out civilization.

The Communistic idea is, and never has been, anything but a carrot on a stick tied to the back of the "have-nots" of the world. It leadeth them beside the troubled waters of endless slavery and protecteth them from naught. And then Communism went belly up. But all evidence be damned! Millions of people, particularly the "have-nots," even here in America, still are dreaming of sharing the pie that never materializes. Go figure some way to prove to me they are sane.

In the long ago Roman Empire, and all over Europe for many centuries thereafter, the thrones that held absolute power over the various people, was a "God Given" inheritance. Incestuous marriages were many, for the "chosen" blue blood lines of royalty had to be maintained. The fact that many of these "God chosen" pure blood royals proved to be incompetent wastrels, causing many unnecessary problems for their subjects, made no difference. At least twice in England, a slobbering idiot was crowned, and "ruled" until his death. But who could cross the will of God? During these centuries, the real power behind the thrones all over Europe and England, were the Catholic Priests. It made their absolute control easier when an unstable moron was King . . . and it was mostly through their constant brainwashing of the public concerning "God Ordained" Rights to Rule, that the masses were kept under the system. God's Will was eventually thwarted and the systems began to change, though that isn't the point we seek.

But it does bring us to this. Down through history, in almost duplicate coups, when a long established religion or Government has been overthrown, it's usually been ONE person, who inspired the mobs to action. In every case that I have been able to study, these various individuals gained the crowd's approval and stirred them to action by "telling them what they wanted to hear."

We've already briefly looked at several cases of this. Let's now look at an example set by one man in the messy, corruption bloated old town of Mecca. His case, while following directly in the foot steps of Gautama and K'ung, proves the point even further, because first, he tried to tell the people what they *didn't* want to hear. That Modus Operandi succeeds with people in the same manner as trying to float a brick.

First, I believe we should take a look at one of the "readings" right out of the Koran. It is the most convincing way I know of to understand the idiocy in any and all "Holy" Books.

"Abraham was not a Jew or a Christian, but he was an upright man, a Moslem, and not an idolator."

"Moslem" as used in that statement means "true believer." Abraham's "Religious" affiliation was not added to the "readings" until at least 6 to 8 centuries *after the beginning of the Christian era.* The Koran itself was only being born then. Abraham in all likelihood, was a fictitious character to begin with, a mere part of ancient folk lore tales dating back to an era before the Israelites or the Arabic races were even begun. If Abraham actually existed, his era was before and during the supposed destruction of Sodom and Gomorrah, and at that time Yahweh as a name, had not begun to appear in the folklore stories concerning "God." The "name" would be added centuries later. But when Isaac supposedly began the Israelites, and his brother Ishmael was becoming responsible for the Arabic hordes, certainly that era had no Yahweh, Jehovah, Christ, nor Allah, none of them yet invented. In the quote above, the Koran disparages Christianity and does NOT acknowledge Yahweh, nor Jehovah. But a "Moslem" of Allah did not come into existence until the invention of Allah. Allah was invented 500 to 600 A.D. Thus the Koran's statement that Abraham was a Moslem, is ludicrous. And of course they *had* to deny him being a "Jew" for the simple reason that Jews and Arabs had already been sworn, blood letting enemies for many centuries before the Koran was written.

But to heck with the philosophical musings! As they say in H'wood, "Lets' cut to the chase." Play a bit of mood music, Maestro, something like the theme song to Dragnet! Then in sepulchral like voice of dramatic impact I'll say:

Into the quagmire of idolatry, innumerable Gods, all kinds of corruption and depravity that Mecca had become, a very unremarkable small boy was born. We know considerable about his life from birth on for he was born into an aristocratic family of the Koreish tribe. Nothing would have been recorded had he been a mere girl, but as the son of a highly respected house, his history for his entire life was recorded. Much of the truth concerning him was altered after his creation of a new religion, but enough of that has escaped being changed that it can still be found.

But many facts *were changed* elsewhere. *After* his rise to found and teach a new Religion, tales spread amongst his followers about all of the great signs that were given to mankind on the night of his birth: The stars in heaven blazed with a never before seen glory. The eternal flame in the Temple of Zoroaster in Persia, faltered and went out. Temples in other great religious centers crumbled and fell. The earth quaked with great joy, and idols all over the world were tumbled off their pedestals. There were unmistakable omens everywhere to let the world know that a very great man-child had been born to cleanse the world of debauchery, idolatry and corruption. These same weird yarns have spread amongst the "faithful" of over a dozen or more "special" sons either while they were rising to great religious status, or after they became "great" and were dead and gone. Spreading such yarns appears to be a recurring human disease that has happened again and again, nor has it ever mattered which religion or which god was being touted. Identical tales of various "holy" men date back into the past as far as our experts have been able to dig.

(Now decrease volume on the theme song just a bit): The truth of this babe's birth was an entirely different story. His mother was still in mourning for his father who'd died shortly after she conceived. Her aging father-in-law, Abu Al-Muttalib, a prosperous leader in Mecca, took the infant to the Kaaba for christening. Please note that in all Deity type religions, very similar "christening" occurs, committing the child to whichever "God" the new baby's family have been raised to believe in. Abu named the babe Kutam Mohammed. This was a standard procedure throughout Arabia then, Kutam being the actual name, Mohammed, which means "the praised," merely being a complimentary "title." And again, that announces that the babe is committed to the "accepted" religious beliefs.

English translation of long ago names from other languages

change from time to time as updated nuances and pronunciations the world over change too. Years ago when I researched this section of the book, Mohammed was the English spelling of the word. It has been changed over the years to Muhammed, etc. While the original followers were known as Moslems (true believers), that too has altered in some areas.

There was certainly no rejoicing in the household where he was born. Added to the gloom that was there, his mother died when he was barely six. He was taken to live with his aging grandfather. Islamic legend says that the old man kept him constantly at his side and taught him every thing he knew. This is another example of how truth is warped and distorted by Religious leader's nefarious manipulations. The real story is that his grandfather also died before Kutam had learned where the supper table was. At age six, he should have been sent to school, but the death of his grandfather lopped that off too. He was totally orphaned and adrift in the early months of his sixth year of life.

His uncle, Abu Talib, a camel trader and guide for caravans crossing the desert, took him in, but not, apparently, for any altruistic reasons. Abu Talib, with no "school learning" himself, had no use for or belief in the system of schools for kids. He put the small boy to cleaning camel shit out of stables. As the boy grew older, he was forced to go on some of the caravan trips as a working trainee. His uncle regularly traded at the leading markets in Syria, Yemen, Abyssinia, Persia, and even into Egypt . . . so the trips were long and filled with much sweaty labor and hardship. And Kutam was learning to take part in the trading, in management of camels, and in choices of goods to barter for. It was in this manner that he became acquainted with "believers" in both the Jewish and Christian Religions. Neither type ever lost any opportunity to attempt a little Religious "educating" for an infidel, especially since then as now, Judaists and Christians were not exactly "friendly" with each other. Kutam learned all he could about both beliefs, but never committed himself to either. Nowhere in his history did I ever find any mention of his learning anything about the hundreds of "Gods" and their idols catered to in his home base, Mecca.

After nearly 15 years of learning the business the hard way, and becoming very good at it, Kutam quit his uncle and took over the position of guide and steward for the caravan of an attractive and wealthy widow, Khadijah. For about five years he did a credible enough job to make her even richer. And even though she had become 40 while he'd only reached the age of 25, he found her (and maybe her fortune), irresistible, and they were married. His life time of sordid labor with his uncle had begun to pay off. By then he was very sharp and experienced at trading and managing a caravan, thus during the following 15 years he made both he and his wife very rich. He became a respected, prosperous merchant of Mecca and was getting on into middle age.

With plenty of money and affluence, Kutam and Khadijah fled the blistering heat in Mecca each summer during the month of Ramadan. They would retreat to a cave in the desert where he could spend time in the coolness of it, resting from his labors and meditating.

One scorching hot day while he slept in the cave he heard a voice commanding him to read. "I cannot read," he answered. Both the order and his answer were repeated a second time. Then the order came a third time. That time, Kutam asked: "What shall I read?"

The voice answered, "Read: In the name of Allah who created man of a clot; Read: And your Lord is most bounteous, and he teaches man by the pen; he teaches man what he knows not."

When Kutam awoke, he remembered the words. But as he staggered out of the cave, mystified and still half asleep, he heard the voice again: "Oh Mohammed, you are Allah's messenger and I am Gabriel."

He confided in Khadijah, but she could not help, though she did try to reassure and soothe him. (Doctors now know that many people, both men and women, begin having all sorts of weird dreams, *and ideas* after they pass the 40 year old mark. The body has stopped being able to rebuild as fast as it is being ravaged and depleted. Worse still, with many humans, is the rapid destruction of the brain's memory and "thinking" cells. All sorts and kinds of erratic thinking and actions frequently become operative.)

The dreams kept coming as he slept each afternoon in the cave. He became greatly disturbed because he could not write the messages down, for he was often reminded by "Gabriel" that he was supposed to "read" the messages. Khadijah hired him a scribe, a man named Abu Dekr. Thereafter, Kutam would dream his dreams, then dictate the "messages" to the scribe, who faithfully wrote them down. I hope my reader will not have missed what I consider one of the most important weaknesses of ANY religious belief AND the "God" or angel that was supposed to have delivered the messages. Most of the words, predictions, and other "messages" from "God" of any and ALL Deity religions, have been built on some long ago person's "dreams." Burning bushes, voices out of whirlwinds or clouds, donkey's that speak (called "asses" in our Bible), are all part and parcel of the same lunacy. If these things were actually happening 4,000 . . . . 3,000 . . . . 2,000 years ago with Yahweh, Jehovah, or Christ at bat, or 1500 years ago with Allah dictating, they would STILL be happening now. I can't believe a God would give up after only a very few feeble tries with one person at a time many centuries ago . . . then never try again. Most mere humans have got more spunk and sense than that, let alone an omnipotent God.

When the blistering heat of Ramadan subsided a bit, Kutam with Khadijah and his scribe returned to Mecca. Kutam assembled friends of his and began preaching to them what he'd been told by Gabriel. They scoffed and laughed at him. But when he began to denounce their god idols, from which they derived great profit, they became angry, began ostracizing and denouncing him. From a highly respected merchant he descended into becoming an unwelcome object of ridicule. As was stated earlier, Kutam was telling people things they did NOT want to hear. But he really chumped out when he began publicly preaching against the corruption and cheating most of the merchants were practicing to milk the public.

In the midst of all this, Khadijah died. They had been married for 26 years and Kutam was grief stricken. His slumbers at night were continually disturbed by Gabriel, who kept instructing Kutam in Allah's name. During the weary, grief filled days, Kutam would repeat the "readings" to his scribe who faithfully wrote them down. Of an evening he "preached" to whatever audience he could raise.

His "sermons" became more and more loaded with scathing exposure of the crooked merchant's practices. Now he was really telling people what they did not want to hear. They had already been referring to him as "Mohammed," in a leering and derisive way, but now a high level plot amongst the most affluent of the merchants to kill Kutam was instigated. One of those merchants had been a life-long friend of Kutam's and at the last moment, chickened out and warned him. Warned in the dead of night, just seconds before the assassins struck, Kutam fled for his life, he and his faithful scribe barely escaping. That night was June 20, 622 (A.D.) It has become one of the most important "holy" dates to Islam. It is called *Anno Hegira* (Night of the Flight).

Jews count our years from the (Biblical) Week of Creation. Christians number them from the (supposed) birth date of Jesus. Mohammedans (their original title, later changed to Moslems) count time from *Anno Hegira*, usually written on their documents as A.H. instead of the A.D. we use. The city to which Mohammed fled was Yathrib.

Whatever corruption might have been going on in Yathrib, Mohammed had no knowledge of, so that part of his "sermons" was not only informative to his new audiences, it was *vital* to them. Nearly the whole of Arabia made pilgrimages to Mecca and here was a "prophet" and "holy" man telling them how they were being cheated there. Not only was it valuable information to anyone making a pilgrimage, it was worth even more to caravan merchants who went there to do business. With the "Word" of Allah, Mohammed was also telling them how they were being swindled by donating great amounts to false idols. At last he was telling people "what they wanted to hear."

Mohammed named his new religious movement *Islam*, which translated means "Submission to God (Allah)." He added the highly important link . . . a "chant," a rythmic "mantra," the one thing that best stirs a throng of people to emotional response: *LAA ILAAHA ILLA LLAAH!* Translated it means "There is no god but god!" Then finally, something for them to hate, their fortunes being squandered to false idols and crooked merchants in Mecca. At last he had created the perfectly structured Religion.

In just eight years Mohammed was able to return to Mecca. Having fled from it and certain death in the dead of night, he returned in full daylight leading an Army of thousands of his new followers, they armed and ready to fight. The people in Mecca saw the approaching army and fled the city, leaving it deserted. But Mohammed would not let his followers destroy anything but the idols. Mohammed pointed out the first one himself, started his chant in a loud and commanding voice, and ordered it destroyed. That did the trick. The thousands following him took up the chant and began smashing idols. They destroyed hundreds of them.

The town's people were amazed in several ways. First they were dumbfounded that neither Mohammed nor any of his followers suffered any retribution or harm whatever as they smashed hundreds of "god" idols. Next, they could see that Mohammed was NOT punishing them by destroying anything else. Nor was he or his followers attempting to loot or steal. Little by little, a few braver souls crept back into town, and it was quickly apparent that Mohammed was not going to punish or harm them at all. Soon, all had returned to their places; and now they would listen to Mohammed whenever and where-ever he decided to preach. With-in two years, Mohammed had recruited thousands more to his new cause.

Then at age sixty-two, Mohammed died.

So far I have neglected the scribe with only bare mention. His name was Abu Bekr. Mohammed had already described to him a great overall plan to establish Islam as a missionary religion for the whole world. Of course in the middle of the 6th century no one knew just what the "whole" world was. But the plan did include what they knew of it, which was no small thing at all. Fortunately, or tragically (your choice), Mohammed had thoroughly convinced Abu Bekr. Now that man became the First Caliph (Successor). He amassed all the writings, (he'd even written all of Mohammed's sermons) grouped them and created a book. It is called the Koran which means "The Reading." Like our Bible, it has been put through humanity's inevitable "sausage grinder" for centuries. Unlike our Bible, until just recently, it attracted no great amount of interest in most of the world's best experts on religious history. But many facts are known anyway.

Abu Bekr faced one prodigious mountain of a problem that is no longer much more than a molehill . . . hundreds of miles of burning desert sand between far-flung towns, cities, and settlements . . . with no transportation except by camel or walking. Bekr knew that it had taken Mohammed eight long years to convert the people of Yathrib when he'd used nothing but "preaching." . . . and Mohammed had been a very convincing and "inspired" speaker. With an army to back him up, it had taken only two years to convert the even larger town of Mecca. Human nature has never changed. If something works, *more will be better! Bekr began recruiting and training "Hit Squads!"*

The size of a squad was determined by the size of a city or settlement they were going to "convert." The leader of course would be a "preacher" versed in Mohammed's "readings," the Koran. The "false" idols in each town would be the objects to smash and expose as robbing the people of their wealth; The "chant" would be the emotional grog for drunken mass involvement; And the sword would be for any who stood in the way.

The "conversions" began. In the years that followed, Islam was spread, mostly through ruthless force, from the Arabian sea on the south clear to Syria by the Mediterranean Sea on the north, all up and down the Red Sea on the west, clear across to Gulf of Oman and up to Kuwait on the east, encompassing what is now almost all of Arabia. How many people were needlessly slaughtered in this "teaching by pen" is known only to Allah, but it IS known that there were thousands of them.

While this was happening, fanatics in Yathrib caused the name of the city to be changed to Medina al Nabu, which translated means "City of the Kingdom of the Prophet." Today the name has been shortened to Medina.

After its rapid spread all across Arabia, the drive for "conversion" died considerably over the centuries. Vast stretches of Arabia will produce absolutely nothing for the country itself, let alone for foreign trade. Thus for centuries Islam became stagnated and unimportant, a "heretic" religion to all the world outside of Arabia. When oil was discovered in various locales in the country, it was of small importance. Oil had already been discovered in the U.S. but was not in great demand. Henry Ford's "horseless carriage" was, for the most part, still a laughing stock. This began to change with his upgrading it to the "Tin Lizzy," (Model T) and his efforts to produce a car that almost any one could afford. As the Lizzy began to replace the horse, we had oil to spare (so we thought). Oil was squandered and wasted for decades as if there was no tomorrow. The Great Depression knocked the whole world flat on its back for years. I doubt seriously if full recovery would have ever happened if mankind was capable of staying at peace. World War Two created *DEMAND!* And everywhere, all over the world, people were fed up to their ears with trying to eke out a living from nothing, and with nothing. The war was panacea, elixir, a "potion" to start the life blood *money* to flowing again.

War is a many facetted thing. Omitting at this time the downside of the insane conditions of war, we must however take due note of some of its other effects too. For one thing, it creates a mad, all out stampede not only for *more* weapons, but even more importantly, for *better* weapons. The war was responsible for the rapid advancement of technology, more so in a very short time, than would have been accomplished in a world of peace in many centuries. But peace did not come with the end of World War Two. So the mad scramble for bigger and better weapons continued to multiply the pressure for technological advance. The human race has developed more in its technologies just during my lifetime, than it had in its entire history before. It is tragic that we did not also develop immunity to emotional bullshit at the same time, particularly *religiously* activated emotionalism. Emotionalism effectively castrates intelligent thinking and conditions its victims into becoming very like robots activated by an electrical surge. The robot or the human will thus "perform" mindlessly, but with predictable results. Go attend a "Rock" concert for an ideal example. When you have that scene etched firmly in mind, attend a regular service in any church you choose. In either visit, you should begin to recognize exactly what I've just described. At rock concerts, sports events, political rallies, Union strikes, Catholic Masses, and Protestant Worship services, the attendees all leave their minds at home. Emotionalism makes all such gatherings successful by the same principles that fucking, fighting, or binging on alcohol does. Humans, through their entire history, have apparently *needed* periodic emotional eruptions. ANY plan that will get a mob together and *give* them that emotional binge, will (and does) succeed. Billy Graham used it successfully all over the world for decades, his "emotionally titillated" flocks loading the hats every time he had them passed around for donations. Rock and Roll "Star's" identical modus operandi milks millions from their "worshippers." Go watch a professional Soccer Game, or the Indy 500 . . . then consider your OWN "highs." What turns you on enough to "donate" your own hard earned cash?

After WW II, and the stupidity of the Korean and Viet Nam fiascoes had taken their toll, the ever present threat and spread of Communism's world take over, or holocaust if they were pushed too far, faced us with some very real and dangerous problems. During this flirtation with Global annihilation our giant oil barons began to be aware of another great fiasco they themselves had committed. The East Texas Oil Fields *had been* the richest and biggest oil resource ever known about. But for nearly a hundred years both oil and natural gas from that area had been both wasted and used as if the supply was endless. Deep beneath the surface, huge oil deposits have great gobs of gas with them. Today that gas is at a premium; just take a look at your own gas bill for using a few cubic feet of it. But for nearly a century, oil barons considered the cost of piping the stuff to other towns to be a waste of time and money . . . . SO . . . . they piped it out a few dozen yards from each well, turned the pipe up into the air, and lit the gas . . . to get rid of the stuff. All over the entire East Texas Oil Fields, literally thousands of these unattended and wide-open pipe flares burned night and day, right around the clock, 365 days a year. This went on year after year for decades. There is no real way to calculate how many billions of cubic feet of Natural gas were destroyed, for no logical reason whatsoever. But besides the utterly ridiculous waste there were two more evils to the absurd handling of it. For one thing, that gas cannot ever be replaced, and was far more expedient to use, and easier to get, than ANY other energy source yet discovered. Yeah, that includes coal, hon. Despite what "apologists" and "officialdumb" preach now, coal cannot hold a candle to natural gas for smelting, heating, cooking, generating electricity, and at least a dozen other drastically needed energy uses.

I've blamed the Oil Barons, and rightfully so. But they in turn, also managed to bribe Government Officialdumb to enact laws that greatly aided and abetted the squandering and slaughter of our oil reserves . . . for the major bulk of the oil under East Texas, is still there . . . but cannot be brought to the surface nor can it be used if they could pump it up . . . which they can't. With the pressure of the gas reduced too far by letting it blow and burn, the oil was no longer forced to the surface. Pumping it up was already necessary with many of the wells when I was a boy growing up there. But at that time, over half of the hundreds of wells, were still under pressure enough to force the oil up. As the pressure was being reduced by displacement of the oil, the REAL drain was because of the idiotic burning of the gas . . . and so every day more and more wells were committed to the pumps. A few more years and hindsight slapped the Barons smack in the face. The oil that was being pumped up was now loaded with sand . . . AND . . . there was no technology to separate the stuff in enough quantity to run even one automobile . . . let alone keep millions of them going. One by one, then ten by ten, and finally the whole forest of wells became useless . . . with billions of gallons of oil still down there . . . but lost forever as far as usefulness is concerned. Oh sure, there's Alaska, and off shore drilling and . . . there are STILL liars and crooked merchants in control of our own "Mecca."

All the while, hundreds of millions of automobiles are burning the stuff up faster then can hardly be calculated . . . not to even mention a thousand and one other needs and uses that are being served too. And all over the world, dozens of Automobile manufacturers are adding to the congestion of our streets and highways as fast as they can assemble the things on a 24 hour, round the clock schedule.

Today we are perilously close to being totally dependent on Arab Oil . . . .

And Islam perilously controls most of Arabia. Given the huge influx of money all these conditions have created, Islam has NOT stayed stagnated, isolated, and an almost unknown religion any longer.

I spent several months in Algeria in 1943. The Luftwaft was still able to strafe and bomb us, but when not dodging these annoyances, I frequently was able to sightsee . . .

. . . from Casablanca in Morocco clear across to Tunisia in Tunis, for our air patrols caused me to be in many areas on a constant routine of "Milk Runs," frequently spending the night in towns far removed from our regular base near Kairouan in Tunisia. All of Algeria was Free French then, with its own National Bank's issues of French francs for money. After the fall of France to Hitler, the francs from France itself became worthless on the world market, while the Bank of Algiers' francs retained their value.

It is not Free French any longer. The "Hit Squads" of Islam brought its "teaching of Allah by pen." The "pen" had long ago been substituted for with spears and swords. In the take-over of Algeria those had given away to AK-47's, bombs, and terrorism. Now most of those towns of Northern Africa that I walked around freely in, have had their names changed to suit Arabic tastes and the people are in constant fear. Well they need to be. Basically it is Americans' billions of bucks for our "need" to be able to drive anywhere and everywhere continually that has armed Islam for its conquests.

There really is no point in keeping up with slaughters in Jerusalem. Stick around a while and you can watch it in person right here in America. All ready, right amongst us, several thousand mesmerized minds are prostrating themselves on Islamic "prayer" rugs. You will note that their ass is in the air, unprotected, and their foreheads laying on the rug. What very few people understand is that this has been the universal submission position for the female of nearly all of the animal kingdom for millions of years . . . she is, in other words, allowing herself to be fucked. When a young male challenges an older one who is "boss" of the herd . . . which ever loses the fight assumes the same position to save himself from being killed by the winner. Nor does that always save him . . . .

There is one other glaringly obvious truth concerning those prostrating themselves to Islam in America. Like Communism, Islam appeals to the poorly informed. Very few of the soldiers and terrorists who "screwed" the Free French in Algiers, could read their own Koran. Thousands of the people bowing down on their "Prayer" rugs here in America are functionally illiterate. Worse they have little idea of how our Government is supposed to work. They have extremely warped opinions of what Freedom really is, and not the slightest idea in the world of what it takes to keep it. But you had better believe that real fire is built under their tails when the polls are open to decide our future. There is very little effort being made at all to get educated, working people to go vote too. In the primaries held in this year 2000, only twenty percent of the registered voters even bothered to vote . . . and many thousands, even including many college graduates, have never bothered to even register . . . let along vote. Have you bought *your* "prayer" rug yet?

Most Americans consider such things only vaguely. "It can't happen here," as pertains to *any* enemy or governmental takeover, has been an unchangeable attitude of most people in our country for centuries. Yet the bulk of these same people have no idea whatsoever about the continual massive effort it takes to *keep* freedom . . . NOT just on the part of our Military, but on the diligent and continual participation of every citizen.

A week after Reagan chose Bush as running mate for vice-president candidate, in a fully televised acceptance speech at the highlight of the Republican convention, several Nationally known news agencies conducted on the street questionnaires of passing adults. Their question was simple and to the point: "Who is George Bush?" Nearly twenty percent thought he was the guy that made beer. Nearly ten percent thought maybe he was a "star" ball player of some kind (actual answers were that vague). Just eighteen percent of the hundreds questioned gave the right answer, but further questioning of those who did answer correctly showed they knew almost nothing else about him. It is this "So what?" attitude of the majority of our people that has allowed our government to become the "God Father" type colossus that it now is and which our Constitution clearly forbade it ever becoming.

The cornerstone, the very life-blood of our Constitution is its First Amendment. For over a decade now, there has come to life a growing and massive effort to *change its wording!* Woe be to all of us when that utterly stupid deed is accomplished!

No one likes to be slapped in the face . . . . and I have just slapped several million citizens hard . . . very hard. I've slapped all of those who are fighting for the change. I do not apologize for the act. They have been convinced that a "litle censorship" is greatly needed to protect "the children," as well as not to out-rage their own Religiously hypnotized ideas of what is not "decent." One of the things they do not understand is that there is no such thing as a "little censorship," just as there is no such thing as being "a little bit pregnant." The clamor to cripple our First Amendment is eagerly sought by many of our congressional "misrepresentatives," who would like nothing better than to have a "legal" way to keep the media from exposing their nefarious dealings.

In fact, I'm ready to slap all of those misguided agitators even harder. You are invited to come along for the party . . . but . . . uh . . . I think you should be sure your seat belt is snug and secure.

CHAPTER SIX

Since colonists braved unknowns to venture across uncharted seas and settle in a wilderness, this has been known as a Christian land. Today there are more churches, more Priests and Preachers, and more "Christian" agitation in our borders than in any other Nation in the world. It is dogmatic Christian pressure that has convinced millions of our people that we need to change the First Amendment of our Constitution . . . . for its guarantees of Freedom of Speech and Freedom of Press have become offensive to them. Another part of that Amendment they understand even less is the Freedom of Religion clause.

If freedom OF religion does not mean just as surely that we also are guaranteed freedom FROM religion, then the guarantee has no meaning at all! But that meaning Christians never even give lip service to, mostly because they have no real understanding of it. Worse still, they have no real understanding or knowledge of how their Religion began, the grossly depraved history of it . . . nor the original cause, meanings, and results of its chief tenets. Let's begin with one thing Christians have been taught to believe all of their lives, so that now they have experienced "proof" that it is so.

For many, many years Priests and Preachers have convinced their flocks with the "provable" statement that *all humans have a natural need and hunger in themselves to know God!* They tell us that the thing in us that hungers for God, is our *soul*. It is time to trot out the Einstein Method again and look at that *"truth"* from a different angle. It really does need examination.

During sexual intercourse between male and female, a single sperm from among tens of thousands of the things, beats all the others to penetrate the "egg" of the female. From that instant on the microscopic little sperm is in total protection and constant supply of any and all things it needs to survive and grow. Nine long months of total protection and supply indelibly stamps into it the wonders and beauty of having to not even wiggle nor exert a finger to get everything it needs. From the moment of its birth on, mama will also protect and care for its every need for many months to come.

Science has determined that a human learns and accumulates more in the first five years of its life, than it will garner for any similar period during the entire remainder of its life. Then, by a small amount of reasoning we should readily see that this first five years, plus 9 months in the womb, in all of which the kid is totally supplied, protected, and cared for, will and does implant in him a very deep seated "need" and continual "longing" for that "total" care and protection. In later years, memory of his actual existence and events in it for those formative years will be forgotten, but the "feelings" and "desires" are indelibly stamped in his mind forever. No matter how old we get, nor the thousands of trials and troubles we have during our life, those same feelings and needs are ever present somewhere in the back of our minds, while the reason they are there has been lost. Particularly does need and longing for that protection and total care haunt us in times of trouble or danger. Thus, for centuries, the Clergy, mostly brainwashed themselves, have convinced uncounted millions of people that this "need and longing" in us, is our soul crying out to know God. That their teaching of that is a totally misconstrued lie has never occurred to millions of people, who believed it because they could at times, actually "feel" that "crying out" in themselves. The very real and unmistakable "crying out" comes most often in the wee hours of the night when we can't sleep and, whether we can admit or even understand it, usually because we are scared and/or deeply troubled. That stamped in, mesmerized condition of total care and protection, free from all troubles and dangers, is what our mind is lamenting and hurting for . . . . *not for a God* . . . except that Priestly transfer of responsibility in our induced thinking has made it seem so. So much for our *"soul"* crying out for God.

During an especially harrowing part of WW II, when our forces were smashing their way up through Italy, hampered by some of the most rugged and user unfriendly real estate in the world, a determined journalist, Ernie Pyle, insisted on accompanying the front line troops of infantry that were suffering, fighting, and dying for every foot we gained. While most reports on the war were written by journalists content to sit around command headquarters waiting for doctored "official" hand-outs, Ernie Pyle, in the midst of the blood shed and killing, wrote of what was really happening to the unknown dog-faces who were actually fighting the war. He was one man who wrote for the Americans at home, the *real* picture, not just pats on the back for the Generals.

After one especially nasty battle in which our losses were staggering, his daily column began: "There are no atheists in these fox-holes."

Ernie Pyle was the personification of Journalists at their best. Not allowed to carry arms of any kind, not allowed to fight back at a determined and deadly enemy, he never the less stayed right in the worst of the fighting in a monumental sacrifice to show America what the "real" soldier was going through, not the big wigs sitting safely back at headquarters shuffling paper and getting all the glory.

His columns deeply affected all who read them, especially so for those who had loved ones in service. "There are no atheists in these fox holes," reassured several million Christian loved ones back home. I don't believe Ernie himself, and certainly not millions of Christians, ever understood the real meaning of that phrase, and it became one of the most famous quotes of the war. If you but look at the reality of its meaning, you begin to understand what the vast power of Christianity is really based on . . . FEAR!

All of our lives we've been bombarded with biblical teachings that we are doomed to spend an eternity in Hell . . . unless . . . . And we've been brainwashed all our lives to believe that God, or

Jesus, can and will, give us solace and protection in times of great danger. The Bible reeks with stories of deliverance for those who call on Him in faith.

That too, is a crock full right out of the pottie.

Throughout the entire history of Judaism and Christianity, millions of devout "believers" have died hideously while screaming to God or Jesus for help. Tens of thousands of kids storming up enemy beaches and thousands more in fox holes, who were NOT Atheists, died hideously, and cruelly too. Thousands of people are starving to death in this world every day, hundreds of them are children . . . and many, many of all ages of them are devout Christians. Oh yeah . . . Allah is protecting the Islams in Jerusalem; God is protecting the Jews; and Christ is protecting the Christians there. In a pig's ass! Look at what is *really* happening in this world and learn . . . more accurately I should say *unlearn* . . . unlearn the utter crap you've been brainwashed with all of your life. God . . . call his name whatever . . . . has *never* yet kept a single promise that he supposedly made in the (so called) *HOLY BIBLE!* *Not a single one!*

I could cite here at least a dozen prime examples to prove that statement, but for the moment let's consider one that will be glaringly apparent. Take a good look at the Book of Exodus in your own Bible. Turn to its 33rd chapter and read it for yourself:

Exodus 33: 1-2 "And the Lord said unto Moses, 'Depart, and go up hence, thou and the people which thou hast brought up out of the Land of Egypt, unto the land which I sware unto Abraham, to Isaac, and to Jacob, saying, Unto thy seed will I give it:

"And I will send an angel before thee, and I will drive out the Canaanite, The Amorite, and the Hittite, and the Perizzite, the Hivite, and the Jebusite.'"

As is written in that first verse, by the Bible's own oft used repetition, God *did* make those vows repeatedly to all of the one's named. In two other promises of the same thing, He said: "And no man shall be able to stand before thee." Again, in several of the promises, God refers to the area as "The Land of Milk and Honey."

I am sure you Bible readers will recall those exact words. Let's take that phrase first:

The entire area being discussed, all of Judea in fact, is some of the most user unfriendly and worthless real estate in the whole damned world. Burning desert areas, miles of craggy worthless rock, mountains not even worth scaling, and a climate hardly matched for unpleasantness anywhere else in the world. In many of the areas that are free enough from these faults to be tillable, the dirt is so poor that it would take ten acres of it to rust a nail. On top of all that, just twenty miles from Jerusalem is the Dead Sea, the most dismal, useless, and worthless body of water in the whole world. This is God's idea of a "Land of Milk and Honey?"

As we've already discussed, the *Promise* had been repeated several times. In some instances He had *promised* to drive out the ones already living there. (These were the Arabic Nations, which had been inhabitants and owners of the area for centuries.) In other times He *Promised* to send and "Angel" to drive out the owners. And at least twice He *Promised* that "*No man shall stand against thee.*" According to the Bible this *Promise* was first made to Abraham over *five thousand years ago!* The *Promise* to Moses was made (again by *Biblical* reckoning), about 3600 years ago . . . and again to Joshua some 40 years later when the "Children of Israel" had reached the borders of the *Promised Land.*

Well, well, well . . . . If you read or listen to the daily news you'll know that the Arabs not only are still there, but are more obstinately standing their ground than ever; and they are NOT being driven out by Angels or God, nor the combined might of the U.S. and the rest of the (so called) *free world!*

There is more . . . so much more that it would take a whole self full of books to describe it all . . . but we must mention one other part of God's failure: For 300 years, the whole of the 11th, 12th, and 13th centuries, the combined might of the leading "*Christian*" Nations of Europe, with England very prominently represented, mounted four tremendously powerful and destructive Crusades to the *Holy Lands.* The object was to drive the Arabs out.

The *Infallible Pope* at the Vatican in Rome, issued blanket forgiveness to all the soldiers who participated, if in the heat of battle they did a little raping here and there! Please keep in mind that wholesale slaughter, rapine, pillage, and destruction of the rightful occupants of this land went on unrestricted for 300 years, carried out by tens of thousands of armed, trained, and bloodthirsty troops from Europe and England. Yet with all that slaughter and determination helping Him, God was still not able to keep his *Promise* to the "Children of Israel." The Arabs are still there.

When you also know and consider that both Islam and Judaism are "beliefs" boiled down from the same ancient folk lore tales (Abraham, Ishmael, Isaac, etc.), then the many centuries of bloodshed, terrorism, rapine, and slaughter (and it is *still* going on) can be seen for what they really are: *The inability of the majority of the human race to think!* My own opinion is that humans are insane.

So what about Jesus and his *Promises?*

Again we could write a very ponderous tome indeed, for the Jesus' *Promises* are even MORE unfulfilled and all of them patently ridiculous! But for the moment, let's consider one of the most glaring and overlooked failures among His many.

John 14: 12-14 "Verily, verily, I say unto you. He that believeth on me, the works that I do he shall do also; and greater works than these shall he do; because I go to my Father.

"And whatsoever ye shall ask in my name, that will I do, that the Father may be glorified in the Son.

"If ye shall ask anything in my name, I will do it."

This promise is made many times and ways in the Book of John, in various scenes depicting the "teaching" Jesus was giving to his disciples; worse, the *same Promise appears one way or another, again and again in every book in the New Testament!*

For 2,000 years, the number of times that true believers in Jesus have earnestly, and even *desperately* prayed for deliverance of themselves, or a loved one . . . asked earnestly and faithfully in Jesus name . . . and then have seen the prayer ignored, would be a number so long and so great that it would overload the most capable computer we've yet invented. But an even greater number of prayers, asked in Jesus' name and with ardent faith, have been for simpler things: Relief from oppression, pain, disease, injury . . . relief from a cruel life under hideous conditions . . . relief from penury in an untenable area or circumstances . . . on and on the list is endless. So great was the obvious and undeniable evidence that nothing was coming of these prayers, that even the faithful began assailing the Priests and Preachers with a demand to know WHY . . . *Just WHY was neither Jesus, nor God answering their Prayers as promised in the Holy Scriptures?*

Doubt is the beginning of wisdom! And many of the Priestly types fear that occurring in their congregations above all else.

When enough people begin to doubt . . . when enough people begin to question Authority . . . then the Moguls of that Authority *have* to take notice or be toppled!

The Priests and Preachers had no *feasible* answer they could give and still retain their flocks. Still worse, they knew it. And so several years ago, one genius among them came up with an answer. *ANSWER?* No way can it be called an answer. It is at best a placebo; a sugar tit for small minds; a milk sop for those who cannot think.

"Oh," said this genius. "God *always* answers prayers. But sometimes the answer is NO."

Sometimes?

Nowhere in the entire Bible does it say that, or anything even close to it. It says again and again: "Anything you ask in my name, that will I do." "Anything you ask of God in my name, that will He do."

Anyone who observes the human race without the aid of colored glasses for any appreciable time, knows that it becomes more and more difficult to understand how great numbers of them can find their way home at night. Detailed study of human history clearly reveals that in all the centuries of human existence, the "majority" has seldom, if ever, been right about anything. Our entire panorama from earliest forebears until the present generations has been one long orgy of wars, rapine, hatred, prejudices, intolerance, and ill will. Open any page of history anywhere and visit our many transgressions and departures from common sense. Added to this tremendous overload of inexcusable folly, we must also penalize humanity for its more than a thousand "gods" he has sacrificed his labors, money, ardor, belief, and (by the millions) even his lives to. Today there are still thousands of diversified "sects," denominations, and "beliefs," in Christianity alone, each group believing theirs is the only right one. Patently asinine are the considerably different ritualistic practices in any of them. Then remember all of the different "godly" religions man has embraced. Intelligent species? Omit our technological advances of the past two centuries and homo sap is little advanced from his earliest ancestors. His basic nature and gullibility are still identical with the "gatherers."

Archeological experts have outlined a very clear-cut, provable trend in our earliest humans that definitely seemed headed in the right direction. They have proved that from the time he began to ingest meat as well as vegetation, his brain size and ability to use it increased rapidly. Homo Erectus, Neanderthal, and Cro Magnon all quickly gave way to Homo sapiens . . . . and there the human race stagnated, still holds itself rigidly in that rut. It has also been proved that until the advent of Homo sap, even the earliest types were bereaved at death of a loved one. They worshipped all things in Nature as the embodiment of "spirits." These "spirits" demanded nothing sex wise, so . . . all genders enjoyed it with any available mate that happened to be handy . . . whether such union was incestuous or with a total stranger made no difference . . . sex belonged to everyone. But regardless of how you feel about sex, whether you relate to it or abhor it as reprehensible sin, see the truth in the many evidences before us. In days of the "gatherers" the entire worldly population of their kind was very small. Many small tribes consisted only of one family and were frequently isolated from other tribes by very difficult terrain and life threatening dangers galore. Mortality of infants and the women trying to have them was monumental. Ignorance, lack of understanding, inexperience, et al, in these early clans was almost beyond our ability to comprehend. Yet, despite all odds to the contrary, *they did multiply and survive!* Few people have ever thought of it, but the multiplying and survival was the lesser phenomena . . . merely the chorus line backing up the main act!

To my knowledge *no one* has as yet turned the spotlight on the real star of the show. Worse still, our failing to do that, has kept the real villain of the ages from being recognized. Just follow the yellow brick road:

During all the many centuries when these totally unenlightened savages considered sex with anyone and everyone to be their only relief and amusement . . . when sex between an adult and a willing child was merely a part of life; when sex between mother and son, or father and daughter, or brother and sister, was all just part of reality: Mark ye well: *Humanity was evolving to become a higher, more capable, and more intelligent species!* And then calamity struck! Some self-aggrandizing son of a bitch invented *Gods!*

The invention of a god, or even of multiple gods (which certainly happened) would not in itself have been disastrous, if such being(s) became merely a totem to dance and frolic before as a "symbol". of joy and life. But the P. T. Barnum types that invented gods had other fish to fry. The fish they did want can be described as nothing less than a ravenous barracuda or killer shark. Gods were invented for no other reason than to *control people and milk them continually!* Through the centuries the names and powers of the gods have been legion, but even casual acquaintance with any of them, or all of them, shows one never ending, never varying trait. Absolute control *had to have a club that could be applied to anyone and everyone! Sex is that universal cudgel!*

Controlling sex therefore became an absolute necessity for the success of any god! A god who had no control over any sizeable number of the people supposed to be subservient to him was worthless. One of the prime necessities for controlling sex *had to begin by controlling women.* Thus women became *property*, given to man by God.

For all the centuries before the invention of sex controlling gods, there had been no stigma, no fear, no rape, no killing, no hatred because of sexual unions. Homosexuality, lesbianism were just part of all the good times. Zoroaster was one of the early birds to perceive that homosexuality would not produce tax-paying citizens, so the practice was declared a "sin" punishable by death. Any one engaging in homo activities, or even making an attempt to, became regarded as a being too "queer" and obscene to be allowed to live. But again, note well: Zoroaster made no mention whatever about lesbianism, pro or con, for the simple reason that a bit of same sex dalliance on the part of the ladies did NOT keep them from having children when fucked by a man. He deemed it better for them to relieve their sexual needs with another woman, rather than cuckolding their husband and maybe causing loss of a tax-paying citizen because of a jealousy caused murder. Centuries later, Yahweh, Jehovah, and Jesus, rubber-stamp copies of earlier great gods including Zoroaster's, followed suit. So go take a look. Nowhere in the King James versions of our "*Holy*" Bible is there any reference whatsoever to prevent, nor even scold lesbianism. Yet so great and continually has dogmatic Biblical nonsense been pressured into our masses, that now any whatever type of same sex desires or practices condemns those individuals to pariah status, hatred, and persecution. The loathing, discrimination, actual laws, even bodily harm against any and all humans with same sex needs, desires, or practices, is still a raging battle throughout our land, with a very great majority of our populace determined to outlaw all such behavior both with written law, and forced compliance to those laws. Most "*Christian*" churches bar any and all same-sex inclined people from even attending services, let alone becoming members of the congregation, or of the Clergy.

We are almost ready to turn the spotlight on the star of our show, who is actually the *real* villain of the ages. We mentioned this as TWO separate entities a few pages back. A brief re-cap will focus our view:

Thousands of years of totally uninhibited sexual practices not only kept the human race from becoming extinct . . . it multiplied their kind algebraically, and resulted in evolutionary progress from mere animal until we became Homo sapiens. *All of that was when human kind was subject only to the laws of Nature!* Please keep in mind that Nature has *never* complied, nor worked *with any* of the gods nor their edicts.

Then upon our progressing species came the Zoroasters, Mazdas, Mithras, Buddas, Yahwehs, Jehovahs, Christs, Allahs, and a continuing list far too long and numerous to include here. By these "god's" edicts and demands, women became chattel property, and sex with them became horrible sin, except under very strict, god-ordained rules. So strict and exacting were godly demands that fearful followers began believing that children, clear up until they actually became adults, should be barred from any and all knowledge about sex.

With the advent of these gods and their ridiculous "commandments" the evolution of mankind suffered a miscarriage . . . for we have NOT evolved any measurable amount since. With better diets plus medical advances we do have longer life expectancy and better health. We have at our disposal countless bits of wisdom and truth gained over the years . . . albeit many times that amount has been altered, denounced, or destroyed by the churches and their bigoted clergy and supporters. Church war against truth, facts, science, and wisdom has been going on for centuries, but it became most pronounced after the first "bible" was finally put together.

Attempts to create the Bible were in progress for many years. Thousands and thousands of Ancient writings from centuries past were considered, some were accepted as "God Inspired," some discarded. Most of the writings that finally became the Talmud or our Bible had begun around 750 B.C.E. for the simple reason the "Children of Israel" had no method of writing until that era. When writing ability did finally become a talent of some of the crotchety old "Monks" of that era, invariably they attempted to pan off their work as having been done during the time it was supposed to have actually happened . . . the story of Moses, the Exodus, etc., for example. But . . . until 750 B.C.E., the "bible" was nothing but folklore tales told around the campfires at night. For centuries story tellers had aged, died, and were replaced. Far-flung camps had various versions of the same tale; many had stories unheard of by other camps. ALL of the tales were crammed full of various versions of folklore tales from other nations, religions, and races.

Also we now know that thousands of those original writings had not yet been discovered when the first "Bible" was created . . . and archaeologists have also proved beyond any doubt whatsoever, that many of the tales did NOT originate with or in the Israelites' history: The *Wisdom's of Solomon* for example, were originally attributed to a popular and powerful king of ancient Babylon. The Israelites had, along with many other plagiarized stories, adapted the "wisdom's" as their own. Thus it became part of God's "Holy Word!"

We have conclusive evidence that the Great Dual Society was operating full blast, with a very large membership, seven and a half centuries B.C.E. A great part of that membership were those who were writing the ancient "Scriptural" writings as if they had been written centuries before, thus palming off something to their flocks that was an out and out lie to begin with. There were the "Priests" of the day, preaching this bull shit to their flocks and insisting on great repentance (in the form of sacrifices of usable goods), for any "sin" committed against the preachings. And there were the "faithful" themselves who usually, by their own guilty knowledge, had to come up with much to "contribute" as sacrifices to atone for "sinning."

Ironically, today's "believers" are still hooked on the identical farce. We have discussed some of the reasons why they are. But in spite of all evidence against "God" that actually exists, they still squirm under the fear of punishment in an eternal hell.

With that brief recap we are now able to identify the "star" of the show. He is quite easily spotted by those equipped to think. His name is "Gullibility." He is smugly content with his own "worldliness," but is usually incapable of, and/or totally disinterested in, researching and seeking truth. "Thinking" is NOT his strong point. He "believes" what he has been "mesmerized" to believe, and would not "think" of questioning it. If some small doubts do assail him for time to time, he goes to his Priest or Preacher, and comes away "forgiven" and convinced. But the Clergy has never convinced him *with truth!* They shackle him with more warnings about having faith then quote for him a dose of *double-speak* that isn't *really* a valid answer. One of the favorite placebos is: "God hasn't revealed everything to us yet. But someday He will when we're in Heaven. Then we'll be able to see why it was all necessary." Questioning ones usually accept such nonsense, especially when warned that they are showing doubt . . . and doubt is unforgivable by God! Biblically, doubting ones need the "faith" of a little child, so that idea is strongly pounded into a doubter's mind. Sure, because a little child will believe anything. He has not developed the mental capacity and experience to do otherwise. It takes considerably more than mere courage for "God's" mesmerized "children" to dump all of this nonsense and assume true adulthood.

But enough of that for the moment. Let us look at the second personality we promised to spotlight a few pages back . . . the *real* "villain of the ages."

To those who do not have to mumble the words with their lips when reading, Biblical text shows quite clearly the origin of "God." Crotchety old Monks writing of "Him" in the 7th Century B.C.E. had no "inspiration" or idea what such a being would be like at all. They copied thus, the only type "Kings" they knew of, *Human Kings!* Now read the "Holy Book" yourself and learn. Therein you will find that "God," as they depicted Him is exactly like the human kings those ancient Scribes knew. If you really read the first five books of the Holy Bible, you will find several occasions where "God," having made up His Omnipotent mind to do something, is talked out of it by a mere mortal human. Noah was able to change God's mind about destroying ALL life. Moses talked Him out of sending he alone to Pharaoh. Lott talked Him out of destroying *everyone* in Sodom. These are mere examples. Throughout the Bible, "God" is continually changing his "Mind" and his Omnipotent "Wisdom" on the strength of a mere human's argument or actions. Nor were those humans ever using "faith" in praying for the change . . . they were merely pointing out a more reasonable "solution" than "God" had thought of.

This point alone should cause much hesitation in wholehearted "faith" in any such "God." But there are other points, iron clad reasons, that outweigh even that absurdity.

The first few verses of Genesis tell us that God "created" everything, the whole Universe in other words, by the simple expedient of saying "Let there be . . . !" And all of it was "created" out of nothing. Centuries B.C.E. this caused few raised eyebrows for many reasons. For one thing, no human alive then had even a suspicion of how unbelievably huge the Universe really is. What they could see was it. Today, with our technological advances we're photographing the birth and/or death of Galaxies billions of light-years away. With all of this fantastic action and its far-flung size, much of the Universe could already have exploded or imploded and we'd still know nothing of it for millions of years yet to come. In other words, "God" did NOT create anything in seven days or any other length of time, for now we know beyond any reasonable doubt that the entire Universe is constantly "creating" and destroying its component parts. Nor is any of that a Johnny-come-lately "theory." These facts alone make the "creationists" and their beliefs, patently ridiculous.

Biblical "creation," according to "God's" Holy Word, was about seven thousand years ago. Whole human skeletons of people who lived thousands of years before that . . . and the ruins of whole cities full of such people . . . have been unearthed. All such credible evidence puts unmistakable lie to the Bible continually.

Humans are accustomed, right from their first startled cry as they are born, to having "limits" on everything. It is practically impossible for our minds to grasp or understand anything whatsoever that does not have "limits" as to its time, distance, size, or extent. To imagine a Universe that *has NO limits in size, age, extent, or content, is an impossibility for most mortal minds!* Try to describe such a Universe to most people. They will smirk and ask, "Yeah? And what's outside of that?"

But of all things that *must* have limits to most people, it is time itself. Tell them that the Universe and life have *always* existed, and they will peg you for being crazy. Very few human minds can grasp, or even give lip-service to such a never begun, never ending existence. Yet these same people do not bat an eye at Biblical threats of an eternity in hell, or promises of an endless bliss in heaven. Their God would also have to be timeless, with never any beginning. They won't even try on that one. "God said it," they'll tell you. "The Bible says so, therefore it has to be true." That is the smug answer you'll get, even though they cannot in any manner whatsoever understand timeless forever.

Even though there are many Freethought protagonists who accept the concept of a timeless existence of the Universe and the ever-changing life forms in it . . . I seriously doubt any human mind really being able to understand it. We simply cannot conceive anything that has absolutely NO limits, no beginning, and no ending. Forever is thus a meaningless word that people use and accept because it has become a part of our language. It is not a part of our understanding.

Try it this way: No matter where you are at the moment, and no matter what you are doing, nor how old you are, you are exactly in the middle of eternity . . . for eternity has NO end, at either end! Therefore, the *middle* point in eternity moves right along with you as time passes. You were at the exact middle of it 10 minutes ago, or 50 years ago. You will still be at the exact middle of it 10 minutes, or a hundred years from now. Don't blame me, if, in trying to understand that, you wind up sulking in a corner and sucking your thumb. It *is that kind of problem.*

So what about all those "saved" souls who are waiting for God's promise of an eternal Heaven? Oh yes, a life of total ease, with no problems, worries, danger, fears, nor struggles. (The womb?) God will wipe away all tears and his saved ones shall glorify Him forever. As a suggestion of what this would be like, read Revelations in your own Holy Bible. As the description is given in that abstract, unrealistic portrayal, should it become real, there is not a human that has ever lived that could be content there even a few weeks . . . let alone endlessly forever. No life form on this earth, and especially the human kind, has ever thrived and succeeded except through challenge, struggle, toil, and seemingly insurmountable problems. Those born with a silver spoon in their mouths, who never have to know the agony of struggle and defeat, never do really amount to much. Their names and fame may become legendary. With worshippers at their feet they may seem to reek with things humanity struggles for . . . but if they have not had to earn it themselves, the hard way, most frequently they are grossly unhappy and disturbed beings. A few months in the Biblically described Heaven would become as boring and painful as the worst kind of life here on earth. The reason humans strive for that fantastically impossible realm is NOT desire for it in itself, but to escape the Biblical alternative!

And that horrible alternative is what we should now look at most carefully.

According to the Bible, that sea of eternal fire is hotter and more painful than mere earthly fire. Worse, a soul can never die there, but go on and on endlessly forever screaming in mind busting pain and torment . . . nor can anything or any power ever give him even a modicum of ease, let alone escape.

Now let us suppose this is all true. A very pertinent question immediately arises. WHAT POSSIBLE REASON COULD THERE BE TO EVEN THINK OF SUCH PUNISHMENT, LET ALONE ACTUALLY CREATE IT? AND WHY SHOULD IT BE INESCAPABLE AND HORRIBLY FOREVER?

But by all means consider that totally!

The Book of Life, described or mentioned several times in Biblical Scripture, contains *only* the names of those "saved" souls who have been "saved" by Jesus. There are many things wrong with just that part of it. Remember the verse where Jesus says to

God, "Not one have I lost that Thou givest me, since the foundation of the earth." Woooo! Predestination stuff! Read some more and you will find: "Many are called, but few chosen." This is a TV game show? But to heck with all the intermediate stuff, however sick it may be. Look at the really illogical God-speak in Revelations: "And all whose name was not found in the Book of Life, were cast into the sea of fire." Particularly notice that the Bible says ALL, which means, as we've already discussed, that those who merely lacked "faith" but never did anyone harm, get equal punishment with the worst and most evil humans who ever lived. Justice? Compassion? Integrity?

The above statements are repeated several times, in various ways in the Book of Revelation, and even in the main four Gospels. Read it for yourself and you can't miss them. However, exact location of any one quote from the Bible is not important for the moment. There IS something vitally more important.

Nowhere in the Bible can you can find ANY justification anywhere for condemning any and all souls who weren't "saved" to the same punishment!

The human race has had all degrees and all shades of criminals, murderers, rapists, sadists, liars, and cheaters. We have also had honest, educated, and informed people who did not and could not believe in Religious blather . . . but who never knowingly harmed anyone for any reason. Put it this way: K'ung fu tze never harmed another human in any way in his entire lifetime. He used his life to try to help others, often with no compensation what ever. Yet according to the Bible, he too will roast forever in Hell, the identical same punishment that the most depraved, sadistic rapist and killer will get.

Go on and think about it. Should I, should YOU, get the same identical eternity of punishment that de Sade, Hitler, or the worst of our serial killers will be condemned to? No explanation ever dreamed up can justify or make reasonable this totally gross and bizarre judgment told of in the "Word of God!"

But before discounting and disbelieving the absurdity, let's examine the Biblical explanation of it. For that we read of humanity's "fall" from Grace in the Garden of Eden. For the sake of examining it fairly and reasonably, let me cite a similar happening.

Once, long ago, I was forced to quit a job, the duties of which had agitated my old war injury to the point of nearly costing me my life. I found the easiest non-physical thing I could locate, though to take the new position, I had to move to another town. My wife and I had seven children, all the way from diapers on the youngest to the beginning of lipstick use by the oldest. I spent a couple of months locating a house near both a high school and one for the beginners. I found an ideal location, three blocks from a grade school, and four blocks from a High School.

The place I found was a nice little brick home with a large back yard . . . ideal in every respect except there was no fence. I hired a helper and we fenced the big back yard, making it purposely constructed to keep kids safe inside and roving dogs out. But that was only the beginning. We boxed in a small square and created a sand pile. We set out several young fruit trees, made a couple of swings and a seesaw. I made for those kids their own safe little garden of Eden, complete with flower beds and all.

But alas! I have no Godly wisdom. It never once occurred to me to also put in the little safe haven any poisonous tree or dangerous snake. How very stupid of me!

I certainly am not the first person to begin considering Biblical writings in a doubtful manner. I am not the first to point out some of the illogical points, conditions, and episodes it continually portrays. The startling fact to me is that so very few have read it in that manner . . . and that so many countless millions have accepted it hook, line, and sinker. But for the moment, let's consider the "Fall From Grace" a bit further.

After the Protestors became too much for Catholicism to ignore any longer and the Inquisition had to be toned down in its insane slaughters . . . the rank and file people finally began learning to read. Wasn't it Abe who said: "You can fool some of the people all of the time. You can fool all of the people some of the time. But you can't fool ALL of the people ALL of the time." That began being visible due to Protestant insurrections against Catholicism. But as this growing herd of people questioned Papal "Infallibility," at least some of them, after learning to read, began to see the same type weaknesses in Biblical writings as I have been pointing out above. Such doubts and unanswered questions are very like a contagious disease. Left untreated a contagious disease can, and frequently does, become fatal to the afflicted person. The same thing applies to Governments, Business Enterprises, and Religions. When doubt begins festering in the minds of too many "customers," the "management" had better begin damage control. If they don't counter-act the growing doubts and regain public confidence, they are doomed to go belly-up in a very short time.

Over the past century, more and more people have slowly awakened, or been caused by others to look at many of the things in the Bible that won't hold water. The Garden of Eden story is one of the things that leaks like a sieve. But it shows the nature of Religious brainwashing when a wily Priest or Preacher can "explain" away the doubts by "changing" the Word of God and the way He "inspired" it to be told in the Bible. "Oh," sayeth the Clergy. "The story of the Garden is a *symbolic* account. Certainly the Human race has fallen from the Grace of God and we need His Love and Forgiveness. So the Garden of Eden is a simplified version of that fall so that we can know of our need."

Yes, there is that great herd, convinced and satisfied by this leaky explanation, just as they have first questioned, then been put at ease with other placebo explanations explaining away other illogical Biblical fallacies. Doubts concerning Equal eternal punishment for all people NOT listed in the Book of Life, raised danger to the Churches for some time . . . enough so that the Priests and Preachers have had to modify Biblical "truths" on that too. Purgatory, according to some of the "explanations," is NOT Hell, per se, but just an unpleasant place that is totally separated from God.

Another great herd are the Fundamentalists. They stick

staunchly, unshakably to absolute unchangeable belief in the exact wording of the Bible. To them the Bible is true exactly as written and no questions or doubts are allowed to even cross their minds. These people are truly mentally sick and beyond anyone's help. Putting a worm on a hook and fishing with it in the desert sand gets identical results as putting reasoning and common sense into oral or written form and hoping to proselyte a Fundamentalist with it. Closed minds are very barren areas indeed.

We have only considered a bare minimum of evidence in this chapter. We could write many, many pages and pages of equally valid accusations all gleaned from reading what the Bible actually says . . . NOT from what the Priests and Preachers TELL us it says. There are very great differences I assure you. But having presented these few faults for anyone's consideration is only a bit of icing on the cookies . . . mere morsels to put my reader into a proper, thoughtful mood for challenging an even more unbelievably gross concept.

Regardless of what particular denomination or "belief" in God anyone may have, there are NONE of those variations that can totally discount an eternity in Hell for *some* sinners. This assurance has NOT been deleted in any of the various versions of the Bible I have read.

I am a mere human. Certainly I have NO capacity for God like compassion, love, forgiveness, or mercy. But even though I have none of those esteemed assets, I also harbor NO slightest inclination to be insanely cruel, to anyone, for any reason, no matter what they may have done. If I were on a jury where the accused was proved, beyond any reasonable doubt, to be guilty of having committed great crime against his fellow man, such as willful murder/rape of a child, I would not bat an eye in voting to have him executed in our legal fashion. Keeping such a felon alive, fed, and cared for during the entire rest of his natural life is stupid, expensive, and pointless.

But in no manner whatsoever, could I be cruel and depraved enough to commit him to an everlasting, mind busting torture in

Hell . . . with NO chance of his ever getting out of it, or getting it finished and over with. Any being whatsoever, including a supposed GOD, that *could and would* create such a condition, and actually commit *anyone for any reason* to it, would have to be the cruelest and most depraved demon that ever has, or ever will, exist.

And so, dear reader, you have now been partially introduced to the Biblical God . . . who is with no doubt, if *real* . . . the villain, the Demon of all existence and all ages. If He really exists as depicted in the Bible, every human living or who ever lived, or ever will live, is in very great trouble indeed.

CHAPTER SEVEN

Ever louder and continually growing in America is the Apocalyptic warning by Holy Joes of all kinds that "America is a sick Nation that has strayed from God and that we desperately need to go *baaack!*" Pat Robertson, Jerry Falwell, Pat Buchanan, Ralph Reed, Billy Graham . . . Oral Roberts . . . even the Pope. And these are just the top party poopers. From their lofty heights on down through the entire realm of Clergy to the lowliest redneck street Evangelist, *all* of them are screaming that we are living in the "last days," and had better repent and return to God. Just incidentally, the cry that we are living in the last days and that our time is very limited until the return of Jesus on his clouds of glory and power, is nothing new. It has been periodically brought back to life for over two thousand years. Invariably, the absolutely certain times this has supposed to have occurred have scared much of the public into great mass frenzy and preparation. And just as invariably on those many past occasions the appointed time has come and gone uneventfully, leaving the Clergy with the apologetic chore of re-plotting and re-explaining the *great* day.

Let's just suppose they are right about us needing to go *baack* to God. Just which Godly era are they referring to? Surely no sane person could think they mean back into the centuries of total Papal control and the Inquisition. Could they mean back into the era of American colonies when Puritanical bigots branded a woman's forehead with the scarlet letter "A" if she'd "sinned" sexually? . . . when they tried someone "suspected" of heresy or being in league with Satan, tied him to a tree or wagon wheel and horse whipped him? . . . When they hanged, burned, or drowned a suspected witch? Neither of these eras, however "Godly" they were thought to have been then, seem to be very needed nor worthwhile to me. Particularly the Puritanical era might seem ideal to Falwell.

To anyone who has burned a lot of mid-night oil in researching the real history of religions, the only era he might possibly think of that the Priests and Preachers might be referring to, would be those starkly miserable years of the 1930's. I choose that era, not because of the gross poverty and lack of any way to change it . . . which was worldwide incidentally . . . but because our Nation reeked with God, Jesus, Bibles, and prayers. Censorship, though clearly forbidden by our 1st Amendment, was so thoroughly practiced by all our media that a casual observer would have thought that it was ordered and enforced by written laws. It is extremely difficult for anyone born after WW II to understand just how really uptight and "God" oriented this Nation actually was. In other writings I have done, I have always referred to that era in America as God-besotted.

One great problem with howling by the Clergy that we need to go *baaack* to God, is that they themselves have no idea as to when any ideal era actually existed and caused humanity to be any whatsoever better off. The reason they cannot refer to any actual era when "Godly" conditions were ideal is because *no such era has ever existed. It has never existed for Christianity! It has never existed for Judaism! It has never existed for Islam!* Bad and miserable eras have continually plagued people of ALL of these Religions for centuries.

However, many millions of people that are swayed by Priestly admonitions, and do their best to *get us all baaack to God*, are missing a number of important effects of their addiction. They seem blind to the fact that the blowhards who are screaming for a return to God, are, whilst doing it, amassing fortunes in the process. These millions of bucks loom even more resplendently powerful and enticing when you realize that the gatherers of it are *not* required to pay taxes on it. Since they are not required to pay taxes on it, they are also *not* burdened with having to keep, or make public, any realistic *accounting* of it to anyone.

Not so strange also was (and still is) the success of Islam leader Louis Farrakhan who several years ago scheduled a 90 city tour in America urging blacks to observe October the 16th as "A Holy Day of Atonement." That of course is the Anniversary of his "Million Man March." As with any other rabble-rouser, now or in the past, such movements are always most successful when preached to the least educated, least self-supporting, most emotional, illy adjusted, and generally the most superstitious people in a country. All of the really successful "isms" throughout history have always started and grown by recruiting these great herds of poorly educated "have-nots."

Month after month, blacks by the thousands were being converted to Islam . . . oh quite peacefully . . . but quite successfully just the same. Then out of the blue came the terrorist attacks on the World Trade Center and the Pentagon. Why the attacks were so stunningly successful is a graphic commentary of how really slip-shod Americans have become in the performance of the jobs they are being paid to do. That accusation is for the FBI, the CIA, the Military, the Air Lines, our Government (particularly Congress), but most especially it is for our people themselves. For all of my adult years I can remember, but especially since WW II, Americans have NOT wanted to be "informed." They want to be *entertained*. Interest in doing a job well is minimal and most people are "putting in their time" interested primarily in quitting time and payday. "What's in it for me?" is the theme song of most American's now . . . . but particularly is it the Bible and Religion of Officialdumb!

When a person gets slapped hard, his first reaction is to want to slap back. After the terrorist attacks, a very great many people in America began looking angrily at anyone who looked foreign, particularly if he seemed to be Asian or Arabic in appearance. So what happened? Immediately great effort was made to assure us that the Islamic "faithful" in America were *not* terrorists and had no militant aims against us. Undoubtedly this can be true with most of the recent recruits into Islamic belief here in America. It may even be true with some Islamic devotees from other countries.

BUT IT IS A PROVABLE LIE FOR MOST OF THE ISLAMIC
FAITHFUL!

Those who are insisting that most Islams are *peaceful, law abiding
types* are either NOT informed on the truth of Islam, its Koran, its
practices, beliefs, and history, or else they are trying to prevent
even more trouble in our land than we already are beginning to
have. On sight killings could, and likely would begin occurring
here if our leaders didn't mislead us about the rank and file Islam
believer. But regardless of what our Government says or does in
trying to dodge and off-set the very real danger that threatens
Islamic adherents already in America, sooner or later, Islamic
slaughtering of Americans right here in our land WILL become
epidemic.

Are the Priests and Preachers right? Do we really need to go
baaack to God? Would that correct some of the awesome problems
we have? Let's take a very close look at a really God Besotted era.
Prayers, the Bible, the Ten Commandments, God, and Jesus were
in total control in the 30's. They were thoroughly and totally
exercised in our public schools right from the first grade on. I
don't believe that in that era *anyone* in America would have even
dreamed of, let alone dared to, question the totally none existent
wall between church and state . . . or the unconstitutional plague
of religious practices in our schools. We truly were so uptight with
religious adherence and practices that we squeaked when we walked.

Briefly, let's take a quick look at what the Clergy and millions
of Christians are up in arms about now: Pornography; Titty-bars;
Sexual explicitness (or the soft-core version of it) in all of our media;
Crime in the Streets; Dope; Alcohol consumption; tobacco usage;
Sex out of wed-lock; Vast numbers not attending church; sexual
depravity in the Oval Office; (And in our Congress persons too)
No Bibles or prayers allowed in schools . . . . Darwinism . . .
abortion . . . The list could go on and on.

Okay. So let's compare that with what was happening in the
30's. Neither our history books, nor any of our official records,
will give you the truth about it. The only way anyone can know

the real scene is to have lived in it. I was ten years old when it began. We had just gone through what came to be known as the "Roaring Twenties," mostly because the "roar" was very akin to the same things that are happening today . . . yeah, "flappers," beer barons, speakeasies, gangsters, protection and/or numbers rackets, and gross crime. People are very akin to the pendulum on a big old clock. They swing all the way in one direction to the very limit, pause, then swing all the way back in the opposite direction to the other limit. Never once, in all of human history, have they ever settled down to a reasonable, happy medium. There is very little likelihood that they ever will.

1936: I was 15 years old. I delivered a paper route. One of the homes I delivered papers to belonged to a businessman in his mid-forties. Most wives stayed at home in those days and kept everything tidy and ready for the return of the "head of the household." This businessman's wife was about half his age, had one daughter in the first grade, and was a stunningly attractive lady . . . with all the right things in the right places. She was very friendly each time I collected for the paper. Home deliveries were twenty cents a week and I always knocked on her door about two o'clock on Mondays to collect for the previous week . . . until the third week after I had taken over the paper route. That third week's knock brought her to the door, apparently just out of her bath . . . and to say she was "friendly" hardly describes the reality.

She smiled and invited me in, holding the door open. It is a wonder I didn't break a leg, for my eyes were not on where I was stepping. In holding the door open for me she wasn't doing a good job of holding her robe together. School kids had a saying for conditions like that: "On a clear day you can see Catalina." Well that Monday afternoon was a very clear day. I did manage to get inside.

"I'll have to get my purse," she said. "Would you like a glass of iced tea while I find it? I was about to have a glass myself."

"Uh . . ." I suddenly realized how very hot and stuffy it seemed. She was back in a very short moment with two full glasses . . .

sat beside me with hers. I guess she had forgotten her purse. She also seemed unaware of the robe and that it wasn't covering up much. I might even have drunk some of the tea. I don't know.

I have tried to remember the exact sequence of who did what to whom and in what order. I do know that I did not seduce her. I was her score all the way. But that is one time in my life that I had the very best teacher any boy could possibly have. She was a very capable, patient, and concerned lady. Gods, Priests, Preachers and Religions do their utmost to prevent Naturalness in humans. But in spite of what ever controls the fate of humanity, this lady had managed to escape from all of the restraints that shackle us to "unnatural" lives. She was totally a *natural* woman, but still made herself appear publicly to be a conformist with the fakery of "accepted" behavior. As a result she was a charming and completely unpretentious human who *lived* rather than merely existing. What a very great shame it is that the bulk of humanity was and is, almost *never* capable of achieving the same norm.

For the uptight, God Besotted era this happened in, the occurrence was even more notable . . . or was it really? Humans *are* natural, however warped they may become under societal and religious pressures. It seems to me, after over 80 years of observation and experience, that most people are very great actors too. Understanding this is the key to understanding and seeing the Great Dual Society as it really is. Far more important, for you, for human well-being, and even for our Country's future, would be for the bulk of our Nation to understand WHY the Dual Society not only exists, but under our (religiously) *forced* conditions is actually *necessary!*

Come . . . get on my magic carpet with me. We'll go back in time and you can visit with me a city named San Antonio. The town is in mid-south Texas, and we are looking at it in the latter half of the 1930's.

Everyone believes that time changes everything. What "everyone" *doesn't* know is that time changes almost nothing! The "change" is superficial, mostly in appearance, a mirage that confounds the eye while convincing weak minds of its "Godly" directed improvements. Reality, whatever it is, has no "directed" evolutionary aims whatsoever.

Soon after my sexual encounter with the young wife, I found it no longer possible for me to not investigate what I had been hearing about "West Side." I heard about it in the washrooms, the streets, the allies, in school halls . . . the only places that kids of that day (and most of them today) could hear anything about sex. San Antonio was roughly composed of four general areas. "East Side" was predominantly black and had hundreds of Negroes. "West Side" began a few blocks from the main part of town and was roughly composed of 16 whole square blocks, perched like a pimple on the main part of downtown. It had predominantly Mexican inhabitants, though people of various other races settled there too. Over a third of the town was mostly composed of Caucasians, though there was no exact dividing line for any of the inhabitants anywhere except for blacks. After Sam Houston defeated the Mexican Army and helped Texas become an Independent Nation, San Antonio became a Military Center and melting pot for people of all races from everywhere. Named after the great leader, Fort Sam Houston was thus a large segment of the city. Air Corps satellites that clustered near, but not in town were Randolph, Kelly, and Brooks Field.

Ah, but West Side . . . it was whore town! There were many whole blocks of shanty's, cribs, shot-gun type small hovels, beer joints, cheap flea-bag hotels, dives, and skid-row joints, all of them too numerous and tawdry to describe. All over the entire area, women by the hundreds, of all ages and nationalities, lurked in every window, door, alleyway or joint, openly inviting anyone who passed by to come in for a good fuck. These open invitations, and the women making them were always on tap 24 hours of every day of the year . . . but of course were scant during morning hours, gradually multiplying in the afternoon . . . and were most numerously present as darkness fell. Lighted signs, music blaring from juke boxes with volume turned high, ready and willing women everywhere, and the whole area managed to look less squalid and men flocked to the "party."

But let's pause, look at more of the *real* scene. Those who know only our present inflated economy with its unbelievable costs and near worthless money will have difficulty understanding the realities of the 30's.

All over West Side, with just about any type and any age female you might want to get in the sack with, the asking price was 50 cents!

All Military personnel in those days got paid only on the 1st of the Month. By far and large, most of them were Privates. (The lowest possible rank.) A Private's pay was 21 dollars a month. From this amount his deducts for Canteen Checks, haircuts, Laundry, Dry Cleaning, etc. decimated that lowly amount considerably. He was compelled by rigid orders to keep himself well groomed, clean, pressed, and shined at all times, thus if he actually drew 15 to 17 bucks for his month's work, he was frugal and careful indeed.

Fifteen bucks for a month's pay! How much partying and playing can be done with that? So on payday night and for about a week afterwards, West Side's 50 cent price wasn't very negotiable. But as the soldiers spent their meager wad and were facing a long hard month either flat broke or almost so, prices on West Side became flexible. I knew of cases where a good solid fuck with an attractive woman was had for as low as a dime.

That is still only the tip of the iceberg. East Side had at least as many whores as those on West Side. They were predominantly black was the only difference. Prices and final deals on East Side were even easier to arrange . . . and oddly enough, the biggest part of the black women's customers were white. Oh, and this was in a time before "integration" had become an issue, let alone any "laws" or Government actions trying to establish it. Ponder that set of facts as long as you like. It *must* indicate something, though I've never quite determined what.

That leaves us the main part of town, the business section. Hotels were practically rubbing elbows with each other back then, especially in San Antonio. Beer joints were everywhere. Premium Beers were 10 cents a bottle, with big frosty schooners of draft easily obtainable for a nickel. When I was sixteen, no beer joint anywhere ever asked my age or for any ID, nor ever refused me service, and it was ditto at any merchant selling cigarettes. After I got my paper route and was making 8 cents profit each week from a paying customer, I still saved money by buying nickel bags of tobacco and rolling my own. Only on very special occasions did I splurge a dime for a pack of "tailor made" cigarettes. One could get a nice hotel room in the "middle class" hotels for a dollar a night and even first class ones had beginning prices at about two bucks a night. Any Hotel anywhere then had room service . . . and any Bell Boy in any of the hotels could have a girl in your room in usually less than five minutes. Her price in most places was a buck for a standard quickie and sometimes as little as 5 bucks to spend the night with you.

In almost any of the down town beer joints, certainly on the sidewalks near any of the hotels, "ladies of the evening" strolled or lolled with-in easy reach. All of them anywhere would "negotiate." All of them made it abundantly clear to any passing male just what could be had . . . and though in that era money was a very scarce thing . . . ALL of the ladies everywhere, kept themselves as attractive and well groomed as it was possible for them to do.

Maybe as this picture has become clear for you, the thing uppermost in your mind is "where was the law?" Certainly much of what was an actuality then was illegal. And I hope you've kept in mind that this was the most God Besotted era imaginable.

Certainly I have painted a picture that appears warped, incongruent, and illogical. Unfortunately it is *not* just the picture that is so foul. The era itself was in far worse condition. Thus, I can present a few of the facts that were factors in distorting our lives right in the middle of one of the most God-besotted eras we've ever had.

For one thing, Government in that era was NOT meddling in, dictating to, nor competing with private businesses as they are doing now. Another thing, regardless of the type of job, pay, or load of work demanded then, it was only a complete damned fool that would risk losing it. That certainly included ALL politicians and all of the Police.

Available women around a place of business have always been good for that particular business. Had a cop gotten tough about running the gals into the pokey, he would have been "enforcing" a law that no one was else was paying any attention to . . . and . . . he would have been looking for a new job a very short time later.

The Federal Government in the 1930's had no interest whatsoever in Prostitution. Any "laws" concerning it were strictly a matter of "State's Rights." Many states had vague laws concerning such things, but left it up to the cities themselves to enforce the measures. City Mayors, councilmen, etc. left enforcing the law up to the Police departments. And that puts us back to square one. Due to the harshness and penury of those depression years, *no one, anywhere, wanted to rock the boat and risk losing his job!*

But there was a heck of a lot more to it than that. If you consider that the era had NO unemployment compensation, NO workman's compensation, Social Security was not yet paying for retirement, almost NO jobs were ever available anywhere with thousands of people hunting and eager to fill any job vacancy anywhere . . . AND the fact that about the only Welfare going on was a few hard-pressed soup kitchens in larger cities . . . you can begin to understand why no one was making waves. The clergy was spending most of its efforts to convince their flocks of their responsibility to the church's financial needs. I heard the parable of the poor widow woman giving her mite (all she had) into God's Work, at least once a month in Church, and perhaps even more often we were brow-beaten with God's instructions to give at least a tithe. Yeah, money was very hard to obtain.

From all of this many of today's Christians would immediately rush to explain the vast army of whores. "Most women will do anything to see that their family has at least enough food . . . yeah . . . and skid-row bums will be glad to oblige because they have no moral values anyhow."

Yes. I partially agree. But if you settle for that en toto, then you are missing a very great part of reality. I hope I have given a clear enough portrayal of circumstances during that era, to show my reader the truth in the following. "Skid-row bums," wino's, and all of that sort seldom had two nickels they could rub together . . . let alone 50 cents. As fast as that kind latched onto twenty or thirty cents, they headed immediately for the nearest liquor store . . . or, even with just a nickel they could get a big schooner of beer. No confirmed, chronic drinker, down and out on the streets, would ever put a quick fuck ahead of another drink. And especially is that so when he is stumbling around aching from lack of a drink for several hours.

No, dear "apologists." The vast majority of men in the 30's had only one way to get money, and that was to do work that paid cash, even if it was just for an hour or one day. In other words, the ONLY men with 50 cents to spend with a whore were members of "the great moral majority" who had a job and worked their butts off to keep it.

Before I continue with another scene from West Side, first know more about what I called a great army of whores. In 1939 I joined what was then The Air Corps, still attached to the Army rather than being a Force of its own. Trading my paper route for a seat in an Army plane gave me one of the greatest "lifts" (if you'll pardon the dual meaning there) of my life up until that time. By swapping work with a wild cat "barn stormer" for flying lessons, I had managed to get my private license on my 16th birthday, the very earliest the "rules" would allow one to be issued. Crazy about airplanes all of my life . . . my total dream was to finally get in some of Uncle's planes. Once there, much of the training was on cross-country flying.

Those old army crates of the pre-war era were already obsolete and long-time overdue for retirement. Thus our cross-country flights were one way to the designated town where we'd layover for a day or two before hopping off to the next target or the return trip home. As a result, through the latter part of 1939 and all of 1940 I was in towns all over the country. If in the past few pages I have given you the impression that San Antonio was a singularly depraved place then I have erred. What I generally described as the whore situation in San Antonio was almost identical to what I found in other towns and cities nation-wide. Whores, if we must call them that were legion, everywhere . . . and in a nation that literally reeked with God, Jesus, Bibles, and Churches. But not quite are we fully into the real scene:

A few months before World War Two hit us in the face at Pearl Harbor, leaders of our nation began our first Peace Time Draft. Kids just out of school, plus thousands of barely adult young men were suddenly uprooted and scooted off to a Military Training Center somewhere. Thousands of them got their training at San Antonio as the Government quickly filled up existing facilities there and created large new ones all over the whole surrounding area.

In those early days of our getting ready for WW II, the great war by Uncle against Prostitution had still not begun. There is no way to ever know how many young men, newly drafted for service, got their first fuck on West Side, but the number would be staggering.

Most of the cribs, shacks, hotels, hovels, joints, etc. on West Side were pretty much the same. But there was one outstanding place that as far as I know, had no real name. It was simply a big sprawling old frame building three stories tall. It was known all over any Army center around San Antonio by its address: 410 Matamores. (Pronounced as Four-ten Matamores and I may not be spelling the street right; it's been a long, long time) Months and months after I left the area permanently, all over five different continents I got into for various duties to Uncle, I frequently ran into proof that Four-ten Matamores just might have been the most widely known and used whore house in the History of our country. Maybe someone should tell the Smithsonian Institute. Four-ten Matamores was very definitely a part of American History.

Sprawling three-story building. Big, wide open bar on the first floor, blaring juke box, small dance floor. Long halls leading off the bar room with small room after room like a hotel down each hallway. Wide wooden stairway to the second floor where there were more long halls with individual rooms behind closed doors . . .

Another stairway to the third floor . . . some more hall and doors.

In rooms down the halls on the first floor were the girls who fucked for the usual 50 cents, though haggling did no good there. Women on the second floor offered "special" tricks, such as a very dedicated blow-job, half and half, dog fashion, etc., etc. Ladies of this second floor got 75 cents. But the top floor boasted of the pick of women as far as looks, age, and abilities were concerned. The specialty of these ladies was "around the world" for a dollar. Not only were they the top choice of West Side, but all of them were always groomed and clad in the sexiest way possible for them to be. A mere walk down that hall, with at least a dozen or more of these super ladies lounging in their room's doorway and giving the stroller their best come-ons, was a study in what our life everywhere could be like, open, honest, and *Natural!* What a very great shame it is, that society in our world for over two thousand years has been brain washed to believe that sex is a damnable sin!

I graduated from high school in the spring of 1939, and immediately begin plotting and planning on how to go about getting into the Air Corps. Since I was barely 18, I knew I'd have to have both my parent's signature on the documents. Kids were old enough then to be put into war and die for their country, but they were not old enough to vote or decide their own future.

I'd long been trying to get up the nerve (and a spare dollar) to have a look at that third floor in Four-ten. About a month after graduating, when the onslaught of trying to get my parents to agree to sign me into Service seemed to be progressing my way, I sneaked a buck out of my paper route collections. The month was about mid-way between paydays for the Army and I already knew that was the best time to go to West Side. I never forgot the feelings I was besieged with as I climbed those stairs.

No amount of talk I'd heard came close to the reality. The

moment I was on the third floor and looking down the line of women waiting at their doors . . . saw the sultry inviting looks, the provocatively scant finery of apparel, I knew I was going to have a hard time getting very far down that line. But I was determined to look at the whole offering before making a decision. I did make it past the first three or four ladies. I'll never be sure exactly which, but it was about the forth or fifth door . . .

She looked very different here, silky nightgown slit high on one side to show one of the most perfect legs I'd ever seen. There was a lacy see through area at top hardly hiding tantalizing breasts. Instead of the rather severe coif I'd become accustomed to, she'd combed her raven black hair to hang down her back with an appropriate amount of it cascading over one softly ivory shoulder.

"Hello, Jack," soft, husky, a sound that triggered many nerves to tingling in me.

I think I almost swallowed my tongue.

She put a soft little hand on the back of my neck. "Come on in. We can get better acquainted."

. . . . and I forgot totally the rest of the women down the hall that I had not even seen.

Yes, writing on the blackboard, clad in drab "proper" clothing, hair done up in a bun, wearing flat heels, and a very minimum of discreet make-up, she'd always been quite different as she labored to teach us English and its many rules. She taught junior and senior classes both, and I had been lucky enough to be in her classes two years in a row. No one would have ever suspected, as she patiently taught diagramming and correct sentence structure, the *real* woman that lurked under the drab "school marm" appearance.

I had always liked her as a teacher for she was competent and thorough. I had learned more about English from her than any other teacher I'd ever had. On the third floor of Four-ten Matamores I learned more about women and about sex than in all of the previous years of my life. She was an ideal teacher there too, patient, very knowledgeable, and dedicated. On top of that she was really into getting all there was out of a sexual encounter herself. In all of the years of my life, I have never gotten as much value in any manner whatsoever from any other dollar I ever spent.

When I climbed those stairs that early summer afternoon, my "education" was just beginning. But after that I began doing a bit of detecting work. It did not take a very great deal of effort to find out where a great many of the vast army of whores was coming from. I have stated, quite truthfully, that the customers of the "West Sides" of America were mostly the employed men of the Great Moral Majority. And beginning that afternoon on the third floor of Four-ten Matamores, I learned that much of the "merchandise" choices in those whorehouses were the wives and daughters OF that great moral majority. Hopefully these facts will give you a bit clearer view of our Great Dual Society with its cover-ups, disguises, its perfidy, and its reality. In a society forced to live *unnaturally* because of "Godly" edicts, The Great Dual Society arises because of its needed solace to mankind, be they male, or female.

Just as K'ung fu tze observed centuries ago, to govern solely by laws and punishment for breaking those laws, yields nothing but connivance, cheating, secretiveness, and lawlessness. America is proving the truth of that philosophy today even more vividly than did the populace of China prove it then. Religion does it totally. Today, more and more continually, America is thus becoming a "God Father" type theocracy . . . with our "Duplicity" becoming ever more pronounced and practiced. Even so, the misguided years of the 30's really had nothing occurring that isn't just as real and true today. We only "label" it differently.

CHAPTER EIGHT

At what age did you first learn of the word fuck? And then when, where, and from who did you learn some of the things that are involved in the procedure? It is an interesting question. When one can get truthful answers from various people those answers are really a gold mine of information clearly identifying at least some of the reasons our Dual Society has come into existence. We are the scapegoats and victims of a very wrongfully alleged "morality." There can be no real morality in the raising and teaching of our kids if we base that teaching on lies, cover-ups, and forced ignorance. When the truth hurts, then it is time to find out why.

In the 1930's, public schools in Texas had eleven grades, seven in grammar school and four in High School. Strict laws governing age of admission in the first grade made a child's birth date the final deciding factor, thus depending on that date of birth, some kids were admitted when they were six. The kids whose birth date fell after the deciding date, were forced to wait another year before being admitted. Under that dividing line decision, I was forced to wait until I was seven before being admitted.

It will seem ridiculous now, the things that began for me in 1928 my first year in school. I began that first grade in San Antonio at a grammar school that taught only the first four grades. It was a "neighborhood" school in a middle class area and was considered a real "class" act, offering the very best teachers and equipment available. There were only Caucasian kids there and at that age I cannot remember even knowing anything about any other race.

For one brief moment, let me get ahead of the story. The "crash" of '29 came when I was part way through the 2nd grade at the same school. Even the richest and largest manufacturing concerns suddenly found themselves with no market whatsoever and were forced to close down completely. With massive lay-offs happening everywhere, the bottom fell out from under all businesses. From giant corporations clear down to mom and pop peanut stands our economy went belly up. Distraught "breadwinners," many times with a whole family under their wing, suddenly had NO money, no work, and none in sight. My dad's job was one of those that vanished and there began for our family a very long and hard fight as dad searched high and low, taking any work he could get, anywhere he could find it.

By the latter part of 1930 we were moving continually as dad would find a bit of work somewhere else. Many times before I finished the eleven grades offered by Texas schools, our family's moving to a bit of work somewhere else, put me in as many as three different schools in three different towns, in one semester. I got my Public School "education" in approximately 30 different schools, sometimes missing as much as 6 weeks of classes in one semester.

Kids don't get much of an education in that manner. But even in that long ago day, kids that could and would learn were being sadly cheated. Every class I ever attended anywhere was drastically hampered by about a third of the students in it, who were either very slow, or entirely unable to learn what was being taught. Repetition, repetition, as patient teachers were continually being forced to explain and re-explain and re-explain, the dullards rarely grasping most of the material, the ones who'd already understood it forced to endure the endless agony while having their time and ability wasted for naught.

But things began to brighten a bit after Roosevelt took office. Dad again secured work in San Antonio as I was finishing the 8th grade. By the time I enrolled for the 9th grade, I had already been delivering a paper route all summer. We've looked briefly at the manner in which my "sex" education was being forwarded from age 15 on . . . let's return to my first year in grammar school in San Antonio and see how it began.

Every year, soon after a new semester with brand new first graders began, the faculty would promote a "pot-luck" supper at the school. They did everything possible to get all parents and their families together at these parties, a "get-acquainted, get involved" function that was wonderfully joined into by most of the parents. I'd been in the 1st grade for only a very few weeks when the party for that year bloomed, and it was from all appearances a huge success.

Anyone who has ever attended a really big family get together can visualize the scene. The teachers and parents were all very busy impressing each other. The kids quite naturally formed groups of their own and segregated themselves for their own games in the halls and anywhere else *away from the grown-ups* in the main big party room. I fell in with a group, two little six-year old girls from my class, a seven-year-old boy in the second grade, and me.

As with the little girl who'd taught me about our "things" being different, this seven-year-old boy knew how to get us to where the grown-ups would not intrude. His choice of locales was a little girl's toilet at the other end of the building from where the main party was in full swing. This occurred a bit over 73 years ago, but I never have, and never will, forget that night.

I don't recall either of those little six-year old girls being embarrassed, or reluctant to join in the proceedings. Bright eyed, innocently naive, we all sat on the tiled potty-room floor and avidly listened and questioned while a little 7 year old boy explained to us all about fucking. As might be expected, the "lecture" eventually led to a round robin game of "show me yours and I'll show you mine."

There was one notable thing there that night. We even had a bit of trying each other's panties and shoes on, much to my own physical delight, and I expect with about the same amount of exhilaration for the girls. But not a single one of us, not even our seven-year-old "teacher," ever suggested and probably never even thought of . . . seeing if we too could actually "fuck."

Again, none of that was just an obscure thing in a bad town. As shown above, I spent many years going to school all over Texas in big, medium, and small towns everywhere. I was in some of the best schools, and in some of the very poorest schools. And *everywhere* I ever went, I found the same underground stuff going on continually. From the day little kids begin playing with other little kids, and during *all* the years of their growing to adulthood, there is *always* this secretive "society" vividly working among us. It never changes when adulthood arrives, just becomes that more personally private. This "dualism" is everywhere, in all walks of life and in all professions.

And it is, with very little room for doubt, our very great *needs* that create that dualism. These absolute needs being forced into ill repute and non-acceptance by "Godly versions of *morality*" have created and *are* the cornerstone and foundation of most of our Society's problems. Don't ever give any credence whatsoever to that ages old bit of "philosophy" that what you don't know can't hurt you!

And all the while, hypnotized, mindless adults by the millions are clamoring against any and all sexual information or even suggestiveness of it, being available for the herds of kids growing up. Total censorship of ALL sexual meanings and information in ALL of our media back in the 30's did NOT prevent nor lessen its underground existence in the God Besotted era of the 1930's. How much wilder and more pronounced are these secretive goings on in this day of instant communication everywhere? Damning it, preaching against it, even outlawing it, *is not going to stop it!* The only thing those efforts will produce, is an even MORE unsavory involvement in it. No God, No Religion, No Laws, and no punishment however severe, has *ever stopped it! None ever shall.* Don't you think it is about time we tried something else?

I believe that right now would be an excellent time for you to examine your own life. If you are an adult and still have no mate, why? Whether you are male or female, if you periodically masturbate, why do you? Sure, I know. Our "enlightened" psychologists, physicians, etc., now tell us that masturbation is NOT harmful, but actually good for relieving sexual tensions, needs, etc.

Bullshit!

Masturbation is a very poor placebo, made necessary by the confused morass of anti-sex nonsense hyped by Religious "isms." At very best, masturbation is a very poor substitute for real sex. Actually the one masturbating, whether male or female is admitting that it's the best he/she can do . . . and all the while, countless others are doing the same thing at the same time, with identical and very real needs. In a sane society, raised and taught correctly concerning the human condition, masturbation would *never be necessary!* Thus, no one would get hooked on it. The majority of people in that sane society would look on sex as what it should be, rather than the "unwholesome," dirty, and *carnal* practice of "sinning" that religious nonsense has forced it to be thought as. Instead of sex being one of the greatest, most pleasurable and freely acquired assets in our lives, our religiously brain-damaged millions have forced it into becoming a thing of revulsion, disease, unwanted pregnancies, and very great personal risk.

The bad apple contaminating the whole of Society's barrel is of course, Religious "isms." But several decades ago, another misguided group began putting even more impetus to an already disastrous condition. The name of that fool's errand is Women's Lib. Very few women, even those most ardently embracing the movement, know that its original formation was mainly the work of a small group of "dykes." They hated men as "competitors," but not just in the business world. Animosity against men as "sexual" rivals was at the roots of their attack, though of course they always managed to cover that up and sell their recruiting as a "bias" breaking movement in the work places.

"Glass ceilings" became a new concept in our business world as Women's Lib fooled countless women into becoming ardent supporters. Just as most women have been taught all their lives that sex is a "male thing" of disgusting and sinful proportions, so too have they been hoodwinked by out and out lies concerning their being "held back" and discriminated against for positions, authority, and wages of equal status with men. One of the most believed in creations of Women's Lib is about the "Glass Ceilings" held staunchly in place by *male dominance!*

Another favorite theme of Women's Lib concerns "sexual harassment." The clamor and action against so-called sexual harassment has had the greatest impact on all of our lives, everywhere. There is scant likelihood of its ever becoming the problem it has become, had it not been waved before women continuously in the same manner, and with the same results, as waving a red flag in a bull's face would have. Without thinking, and frequently with little or no actual provocation, women in all sorts and in all kinds of offices and jobs everywhere, have brought sexual harassment lawsuits against male members in the same offices and jobs. Some of it is even justified.

We'll look at the justification examples first.

Very few men (percentage-wise) have any notable attractiveness. As would be paramours they are more frequently than not, mere blobs. Nor is all of that great lack just in looks only. Their main negative aspect of "persona" is the "boob-Mc-nut" approach to any nearby female. These men, never taught any truthful reality about sex and its successful gaining, are boors at approaching women, and with no doubt whatever fall victim to believing that to "proposition" a woman is an effective way to score. Oh yes, there is no doubt whatsoever, that sexual harassment DOES exist almost everywhere.

Unfortunately, for uncounted centuries, many women by the tens of thousands have learned that they too can "score" better deals, favoritism, and softer berths with a bit of sexual reward to the guy able to deliver it. This has been one of the real powers of women throughout recorded history. Thanks to Women's Lib that idea has become, for most women, reprehensible and discredited entirely. But they also launched another very harmful trend with their ballyhoo that we have in no manner seen the ultimate results of yet . . . though with no doubt the results are tragically harmful enough already.

All the way from small local offices, clear to the top office in the land, women by the hundreds are screaming publicly about sexual harassment on their jobs. Lawsuits by the thousands are helping to overload our already swamped Judicial branches at all levels. Settlements, judgments, and the conducting of the hearings are costing American taxpayers uncounted millions of dollars, and in private business companies, are many times the final straw that bankrupts the company. But the greatest number of complaints is from women engaged in various governmental endeavors. Police departments are a hotbed for such suits. We've mentioned the boob-Mc-nut jerks. Truly they *are* out of line many times. But with little doubt, a very great number of the complaints are made with little or no legitimacy whatsoever. Like old maids peering under their bed at night before they'll get into it . . . many women have been taught to see "sexual harassment" in a friendly good morning from a male employee or boss when they arrive for work. An admiring look at a female in his company can cost a man his job, and worse. When promotions come up and a woman isn't advanced, she does NOT even consider fairly her own eligibility, or lack of it. She starts screaming about "harassment" and "glass ceilings."

For centuries, scientists have known that "water will find its own level." It seems odd to me that we have ignored and not understood that identical condition in the human race. Always in the past, and certainly visible right now is the fact that some things can be done better by women, than by men. I do not argue with that fact at all. But women cannot argue with the fact that many things can be done better by a man, than any woman alive. Despite that provable fact, women by the millions are flatly refusing to believe it or give any credence to it. They keep screaming and as a result:

Women have been given high positions in our Military . . . . "given," not earned. The main results of this have been ignored or whitewashed over. The chief results of it have been the *lowering* of Military standards. When we are forced into another real war, not just the little skirmishes we've been having with Saddam and bin

Laden . . . the substandard forces we'll have to put against a formidable enemy cannot help much toward any real victory. No chain is ever stronger than its weakest link.

Ah, but there is an even greater buffoonery on the part of our Military leaders. Because of demands from the women libbers, women now occupy positions on naval ships, and . . . of all places . . . on submarines. Not expecting and knowing what will happen on our big ships, many times months out at sea with no one seeing anyone else except their own "incarcerated" crew members is example enough of great idiocy on the part of our leaders. But consider an even worse case. No humans anywhere have to live a more closely knit "togetherness" than do the crews on a submarine. So our military "brains" have put women onto our ships . . . and even more foolishly, into our submarines.

The bumble-buttedness of these placements was and is, blunder enough. But then for these head-honchos of our Navy to hit the fan with surprise and indignation, with court-martials and stiff sentences, every time a bit of sexual activity occurs on those boats, is the ultimate last word in stupidity. It is also a further weakening of our armed forces in all branches, and at all levels. With that kind of "non-thinking" leadership in total control, a real war now might well defeat us.

For uncounted centuries, sex has continually and without let-up always occurred. No amount of "non-thinking" has ever stopped it. As long as the human race exists, it will continue to happen. Why that fact has never been given credence to by the majority of Deity Religious victims is beyond me to understand. Anything of that age, duration, and obstinate continued occurrences should be "understood," not severely boycotted and forbidden. Our true natures should be understood, accepted and taught to our young as the realities they are. This should be done regardless of the in-depth studies that would have to be made to come to a reasonable understanding of our selves. As we began to understand these things, participation in and legalization of our natural selves and our inevitable practices would erase swarms of today's societal dilemmas and problems. Religious bigotry has never come even close to understanding or controlling what is happening in spite of their unnatural "hang-ups" and assaults against it. If their "God" can't control sex, why do they continue to demand control of it by man-made laws? And why can't they see that those man-made laws have never succeeded in doing anything except obfuscating and deteriorating our Society that much further?

However that last question is at best an ambiguity. If the majority of humanity could actually think, Religions would never have gained the strength they have nor would they have kept the gargantuan power they continue to wield.

Consider my sadly crippled introduction to "fucking" (detailed earlier in this Chapter) when I had just become 7 years old. Was yours any better? Of all you now know about sex, what of it is real understanding and how much of it is warped *misinformation?* Do you really even know for sure just which is which?

And what of *your own* sexual life? Is it really all it could be? Just maybe you are being cheated more than you know.

Even a casual glance at statistics in our nation should be enough to convince the most skeptical person that something is certainly wrong with the way we are conducting our lives. Over half of our adults are functionally illiterate. Half the marriages being entered into wind up in divorce. Over half our children are born to unmarried women, thousands of them not old enough to vote. Our prisons and jails are all full beyond intended capacity while courts that handle criminal cases are all operating at a minimum of six months behind because of the overload of cases still untried. All sorts of skullduggery are epidemic in our government at all levels. Worse, this is a quick glance at only *part* of the whole story. A closer, really concerned look should cause any intelligent person to realize that the prognosis for our future, for our freedoms, and for our selves is bleakly disturbing and negative.

None of the long list of worshipped and believed in gods of the past has ever solved any of humanities problems. None ever shall. But if we continue to follow the *unnatural* restrictive nonsense of Judaeo-Christian beliefs, erroneously called "morals," then we are in for even greater societal problems than any of us are prepared to handle.

CHAPTER NINE

When I began believing there was great need for a different kind of book about Deity Religions and their various great I AMs (be His name whatever), I knew I had chosen a subject that would be about as popular as bad breath and body odor combined. Nevertheless, I began asking questions and seeking answers from all sorts of people. One phase of that was done easily, but not without many problems. I would visit a popular bar, get the crowd's attention, then state: "I'm writing a book on Religion. I would like to ask some questions and I promise that no one answering will ever be identified in the book or by me.. All I want is your honest answer. It is a kind of poll I'm doing." Then I would ask the question: "Do you believe in God?" asking it of the whole crowd in each joint. After getting the crowd's attention and asking the question of them at large, I then would give each one a chance to answer individually. I didn't ever ask for any of their names. I conducted this experiment in over a dozen bars, and never got a "No" for an answer anywhere.

This might not appear pertinent to my aims in this book. Actually it is of greatest importance. For I was getting those absolutely "Yes" answers from people who regularly drank and many of them were already drunk when they answered. When you frequent any bar it does not take very long to discover that most of their clientele habitually come again and again to that particular joint. After getting the big absolute "Yes" from each person, one at a time, I would then ask he or she when was the last time they went to church. Asking that question of strangers in a bar is all the way from dangerous to suicidal. But the answers as well as the reactions prove the real reasons of just why Christianity, our predominant Religion, is so strong.

Most of the ones answering my questions in those bars had not been to church in years. Some of them went occasionally, usually on Christmas or Easter. The majority of people in America do *not* go to church regularly. That majority just happens to include bar patrons too. From any poll honestly conducted, and from church records of attendance, it can be proved that with the possible exception of Christmas and Easter, less than a third of our populace is in church on any given Sunday.

With little room for doubt, we can thus determine the bottom line to all of that. *People are afraid to admit disbelief no matter what their doubts may be!* Scientifically this is termed as Psychasthenia: incapacity to resolve doubts or uncertainties, or to resist phobias and obsessions that many of the afflicted know are irrational. It is vividly apparent that most people in America are *Psychological* Hedonists while never consciously believing in Hedonistic ideas. One great proof of this is the mass of outcry against nudity and sexual explicitness in our media. All the while those type shows draw the biggest audiences.

The very great majority of those complaining do NOT know that the Hard Right Fundamentalists have been trying for decades to outlaw and obliterate everything that they find objectionable. Every time they got attention enough to get laws passed against sexual explicitness in our various media, our appellate Courts, even our Supreme Court has declared such actions as unconstitutional. After many decades of dismay by our Constitution's First Amendment and its guarantee of freedom of speech and press, the oft defeated Hard Right eventually tried the only thing that has ever had a real chance of succeeding: They began screaming that changing that First Amendment was necessary ". . . *to protect our children!*" Unfortunately, the bulk of our populace has never considered that censorship will NOT "protect" the children. It will, without fail, make my own childhood introductions to sexual misinformation into the same colossal blunder for the kids now and in our future. Perhaps to even greater disaster, legalized censorship of any kind will be used to "gag" our media from exposing the nefarious doings of unscrupulous political "self-servers" in high places. There is far too much of that happening already.

I have often wondered why so many people look on nudity and sexual explicitness in all our media with such imagined and/or "proclaimed" revulsion. Let us look at a very probable similar example.

Before most of you were born, a Swiss psychiatrist, Herman Rorschach, was waiting for his next patient to enter his office when he accidentally spilled ink on a sheet of paper he'd gotten ready to make notes on as he talked to her. (In those days permanency for written material like his notes on patients were written in ink. Since ball points were still far in the future, permanent writing was made by dipping a pen again and again into an ink bottle. Each dip would enable the writer to jot down a few words, then his pen would be empty and he'd have to dip it again.) Muttering about the accident under his breath, Herman folded over the ruined sheet to help blot up the ink mess. Pushing it to one side, he placed another blank sheet on his desk and told his assistant to admit the next patient.

His interview with the patient was barely begun when she spotted the ruined sheet, unfolded it and looked. "Yetch!" She exclaimed. "Witches. Why do you keep such things?"

Herman looked carefully at the blop of dried ink himself. It looked to him like a poorly done silhouette of a tree. Looking at the revulsion on his patient's face concerning "witches" on the sheet, he remembered that in talking to her on previous occasions, he'd already diagnosed her as being "obsessed" with things she considered evil. So he got the blank sheet he'd just put on the desk, spilled a bit on ink on it, then folded it over to make a new blob. Opening it he ask her: "What is this one?"

"Ugh!" She yelped. "Bats! Hairy, grotesque bats!"

He looked at the blob himself. "A butterfly, maybe . . . crude non-the-less. But bats? Emphatically no!" he muttered to himself.

When the session with the "obsessed" one who saw witches and bats in the two blobs had finished her session and gone, Herman took several more sheets of paper and proceeded to make a few more blobs. He showed these to the next several of his patients and one by one was astounded at what he was hearing. Each of the patients had been coming to him for some time and he had carefully diagnosed their conditions only after lengthy and costly investigations . . . .

. . . . and here in the ink blobs they saw visions quickly verifying that he had diagnosed them identically as to what they were revealing by what they saw in the blobs! He realized that he had discovered a quick and efficient method of diagnosing a troubled patient, without the long drawn out sessions it had previously been taking. Thus the famous "Rorschach Ink Blot Tests" were born. It quickly became a dependable tool for psychiatrists everywhere to diagnose patients without the usual lengthy and very expensive multiple sessions it had previously taken.

Only one major problem developed. Writers, constantly looking for subjects that can be written as salable articles, learned the basics of the tests, and who saw what in them. It was payday for these writers, doomsday for the Ink Blot Tests. In magazines, Sunday Supplements in the newspapers, and in books quickly appearing on the market, anyone could read of the nitty-gritty concerning the ink blots and what various answers meant about the person viewing them. Thus to escape "undesirable" diagnoses, all a patient had to do was answer a doctor's questions concerning a blot that it looked like a tree, or birds on wing, or some other peaceful thing. Seeing threatening Indians, a witch, or any other unpleasant thing got a diagnoses of unpleasant proportions. What had been a valuable tool for psychiatry was thus rendered almost totally useless when a doctor was examining anyone who read the papers, books, or columnists.

What apparently has been missed by most doctors is a startling fact that should long ago have become a very valuable tool with-in itself. If looking at a mere blob of ink caused some folks to see things that were reviling, disgusting, or fearsome, while the same blob of ink caused others to see things that were peaceful and/or beautiful . . .

. . . . then what do *real pictures of real objects cause in these same diverse personalities?* The answer is abundantly obvious. Suppose the picture shown is an artistic presentation of a nude? Some folks will look and see beauty. Some will look and be sexually stimulated. But the biggest number of them will see a pornographic display of Hedonistic filth! . . . ALL of those being tested are looking at the same picture!

There remains little doubt that the really brainwashed in our God-besotted populace are going to be outraged by the picture. Those who have managed to escape or disregard most of the "moralistic" perversions of mind-destroying god-myths will most likely see beauty, naturalness, and a desirable portrayal of Nature's most complicated and resourceful life form. But the picture does NOT reflect vulgarity or promiscuity in the model. It shows the model as Nature created, and still creates, ALL of its life forms, *Natural and Nude!*

Those who look at the picture with only lewd leering and imaginings are reflecting their own warped mentalities. Invariably their mentalities were warped (damaged actually) by the nefarious and sneaky ways they were introduced to sex and to their own sexual awakenings and needs. But even this class of *Psychological Hedonist* is usually far less threat to moralistic reality then their much worse brain damaged neighbors, the unapproachable and unreasonable Christian bigots.

The person who sees the picture only as a display of vulgarity and sexual promiscuity, all the while staunchly refusing absolutely to accept it or any alternate explanation as to what it really is, has the worst case of mental hang-up and damaged thinking in our society. Christian *"Morality,"* has thus become the greatest destroyer of truth and freedom we have. It is the backbone and prime cause of why we have so many sexual blunder-butts in our ever present "two faced" Great Dual Society.

The Great Dual Society could and would become extinct if an impressive enough number of people displayed the courage to voice their doubts concerning religious dogma, its errors, improbability, wrong thinking, and counter-productive actions. In that statement I have uncovered a very great imponderable condition. There are countless cops who will face an armed and dangerous hoodlum in a dark alley. They'll bring him in alive, if possible, all the while risking their own life to do so. There are thousands of Firemen, who risk their lives every time their fire alarm sounds. We have tens of thousands of young men who swear themselves into our Armed Forces, knowing full well they are taking a very dangerous and demanding job. I've seen this type in action when a war actually happens. Courage in many of these men when they are in deadly combat cannot really be described nor understood. But ask any of these cops, firemen, or Service Personnel to openly admit that God is questionable at best, and their "courage" disappears like the dew on a lawn when the hot summer sun comes up. Even people who have real doubts about God or Christ can rarely be drawn out to openly state them. If they *do* voice these doubts, it is rarely in an open defiance of God, but rather, a sort of hat in hand attitude as if they are hoping you will explain away their misgivings and questions.

I have known quite a number of both men and women who have finally dismissed the Jesus story as the hoax his alleged existence was, but after having taken this step towards sanity, they will still believe, cling to, and accept the provable lie about a great God's existence and Supremacy.

For all the reasons outlined thus far in this book, our nation is ever becoming more and more like a rudderless ship in a storm whipped ocean. A very bad and dangerous reef is already scraping at our hull.

A very real Armageddon may already be in our near future. When it happens, and sooner or later it will, our real battle just might make the Biblical Armageddon look like a pink tea party in comparison. When that war starts you can bet your last buck on this: Somewhere behind all the headlines, editorials, political posturing and bullshit, the hate and fury that actually launches a conflict with out mercy, will be for one of the "Gods" versus one of the other "Gods." Hey! Did it ever occur to you that ours might be the wrong one?

CHAPTER TEN

Several times in past pages I have made the statement that the Bible has many provable errors and self-contradictions. This is a slap in the face to many millions of people who have never had any doubts and firmly believe that the Bible is the "inspired" Word of God. Unknown to them most Priests and Preachers shun some parts of the Bible like it was the plague. Instead, they preach sermon after sermon, using familiar and continually repeated verses in the Bible, until the alleged "truth" of it is stamped immovably in the minds of their congregations. When the Clergy *does* quote from the Old Testament and bases a sermon on that reading, it is almost invariably used because it seems to foretell of Jesus' coming to "save" souls. If prophets *could and did* foretell his coming, their action cinches acceptance of Jesus and thus of the Bible's many yarns. The mass of "belief" in the Bible then has come about partly because of ignorance of facts concerning those alleged predictions.

An even more oft practiced ploy of the Clergy when they do base a sermon on one of the old Testament books, is to constantly use verses from Psalms, Proverbs, Ecclesiastes, Song of Solomon, or one of the various other so called "Prophets." When if ever, did you hear a sermon about, or a Clergyman reading from, a few verses of Leviticus, Numbers, or Deuteronomy? You likely never will, and if you read those three books you'll begin to understand why. But we'll get back to those three books later.

In England a few years ago, a large panel of various experts on ancient languages and writings, on biblical history, on geological findings, etc., etc., did a massive, five year study and evaluation of the (so called) *Authorized* King James version of the Bible. And while we are at it, not even counting the *New* versions of the Bible, which according to Billy Graham you should use ". . . because they are easier to understand," there are over 14 *different "Authorized" versions OF the King James version!* Well, well, well . . . indeed miracles never cease. Anyway, back to the panel of experts and their five-year massive study of the Bible. Their conclusions: "There are over 19,000 provable errors and self contradictions in God's Word, The Holy Bible." Does that really sound like an Omnipotent, All Knowing God inspired the thing?

I'm no expert on anything. But I do have a marked ability to read and understand what I'm reading. When I know that tens of thousands of people DO read the Bible and find nothing wrong with it or its many tales, then I have to know there are many thousands of people who *cannot* read with any great amount of understanding about what they are reading.

It is worth stating here that you *should* read the Bible. But that will only be of benefit to you if your read what the Bible *actually* says, *not what the Priests and Preachers TELL you it says.* There is a very great difference, I assure you.

To demonstrate what I'm speaking of, you and I are going to read a few verses together. In this experiment I hope to show you how a bit of thinking while reading the Holy Bible will net you much in the way of understanding why I frequently refer to it as the Wholly Babble. But another of the great problems with religious "believers" is that they almost invariably turn to verses they know thoroughly already, for those are the verses, followed by sermons on those verses, that they have been brain-washed with for years. Many folks have been hearing the repetitions all of their whole lives. Ask them why they don't read some of the books of the Bible they *aren't* familiar with, like in the Old Testament. The answer usually will be: "The Old Testament is too hard for me to understand."

So, let's forget that illogical method and read the Bible just as we would necessarily read any other book, by starting on the first page of the first chapter and reading straight through until we begin to understand a little of the whole reality about it. Everyone, anywhere in America knows something about the stories in Genesis, the first book of the Bible. So let's read the story of "Creation" and the fall of man from Grace and see what it really says:

GENESIS. Chapter One, verse 1: "In the beginning God created the heaven and the earth." Hey, hold it! Let's take a good look at that! If the Biblical God is real and actually exists, then inescapably, without any possible exception, He has *had* to exist forever. The only possible explanation otherwise is that some even greater Power had to create God. Many times in many places in the Bible we are told of the "Heavenly Host." Invariably the referrals indicate that those Angels, etc. had been with God forever, eons and eons *before* the earth et al was "created."

If all of that is true, then there was *never any beginning!* The creation of the "heavens and earth" would be merely a continuing addition, a *furthering* development of God's power. Anyway anyone looks at that first line of Genesis, *it is an erroneous statement!* However, that is only the least of its problems. Witness:

When the book of Genesis was written, no soul alive anywhere on earth had any slightest understanding of the "heavens and earth." What they could see of the "heavens" was merely a moon and twinkling stars at night, a blue sky and burning sun during the day. The world to them was flat, and if one strayed too far out, he would fall off. Comparing their idea of "heavens and earth" with what we now know of it would be similar to comparing a single grain of sand with the sands of a very long and wide desert.

Our technology of today has proved beyond reasonable doubt that throughout the "Heavens" births and deaths of whole galaxies full of suns, moons, planets, etc., are continually occurring. We have photographed some of these happens that are more than four and a half *billion light years away from us!* Our scientists now know and have proved that the "creation" of the "heavens and earth" is a continuing reality that has been going on for billions and billions of years and is *still happening right now, even as you read these lines.* Therefore, the "heavens and earth" were *not "created." They were then and still are now, being constantly and continually "remodeled."*

One other little item: There is no way to determine how far this gargantuan Universe extends, in all directions, for billions and billions of more "light year" distances than it is possible for us to understand. There is no number known to us that would anywhere near equal the number of suns, planets, moons, asteroids, comets, etc., even in one galaxy, let alone in the millions and millions of other galaxies we now know exist. And on top of that there are more millions of galaxies out there we haven't even located yet.

If we now have a reasonable grasp of all that . . . then pray tell me how many uncountable billions times billions of tons of many various types of material it took to "create the heavens and earth!" Yet, according to Genesis God "created" all of that merely by saying, "Let there be." The best scientific minds that have ever existed on this earth have never conceived any way whatsoever, that any material, even just a few atoms of it, can be "created" out of absolutely nothing . . . let alone billions times billions to the Nth degree tons of it! Worse still we *must* consider that the "forces" at work even in our one little solar system are beyond estimating, or even understanding just how they all work and what drives them. Gravity, which can be demonstrated, is not fully understood, and it is just *one* of countless energies and forces that keep us in place and allow us to exist.

I've mentioned here only a few of the things that should prove to any reasonably informed and intelligent person that that first line of Genesis is a very silly and impossible lie. "Word of God?" Nonsense! The statement is nothing more than a remark born out of total ignorance. But it was also coined as a beginning to "controlling" those who could be convinced of its validity.

Let's continue:

Genesis 1: 2. "And the earth was without form, and void; and darkness was on the face of the deep. And the Spirit of God moved upon the face of the waters."

Nothing anywhere can exist without "form." We have no descriptive words for many types of forms, true enough. But whether or not we can describe any form as easily as we can describe a cube, ball, cone, or whatever . . . *anything, everything does have some kind of form else it isn't existent at all.* Void: (Webster's Dictionary) n. Empty space, emptiness, vacuum. Webster's gives more than a dozen similar descriptions, the culmination of which mean "nothing." And look at the last line of verse 2, concerning the Spirit of God moving on the face of the waters. If the earth was without form and void where did the water come from and how did it stay put? But let us not call that another impossible. Let's just say that it sounds very highly *improbable.*

Verse 3: "God said let there be light." We've already briefly considered that remark. However, our mention of it earlier, didn't refer to what all is involved here. The "light" had to be our own sun. This sun is many times larger than earth. It is millions of miles away and is really a very similar thing to the fire and heat generated by a nuclear explosion, or fission-fusion-fission of hydrogen . . . like in a hydrogen bomb, friend. But despite "creating" that "light" being a great strain on probability, there is a veritable sea of other problems in that part of the "creation." The relationship between the sun and earth, to say nothing of all the other planets in our Solar System, is steady and dependable solely because of their orbiting habits with each other and the gravitational attraction between them.

Each member of our Galaxy is orbiting at tremendous speeds, while the whole Galaxy itself maintains its membership in the Universe by traveling at an even greater speed, with identical attractions and/or repulsions for other speeding galaxies. Apparently no Galaxy can do its thing totally independently from the rest of Universe and the countless galaxies in it. That was one whale of an accomplishment then, for God to say: "Let there be," and thus cause the whole enchilada to begin functioning simultaneously. But let's let that one go too as just another "improbable."

Verse 4: "And God saw the light, that it was good, and God divided the light from the darkness."

Friend, that statement is totally absurd. The people that wrote that old tale did not know that (1.) The constant fission-fusion-fission of hydrogen that makes our "light" is one of the most deadly things in existence for ALL known life forms . . . IF they are exposed to it directly. This is true even from the remote distance we get that light. The *only* thing that keeps us and every living thing on this planet from being burned alive is our protective shield of air. And just incidentally that envelope of air is also necessary to convert the massive emissions of the sun into light. Without that air, earth's life forms, all of them, would have been incinerated in a very short time, and it would have been done in total darkness. It is the air blanket and the multiple things in it that refract the sun's burning, searing heat energy into light. Space outside our air blanket, even though fully exposed to the sun, is as dark as dark gets.

But all of that is commentary only on the first half of verse 4. Look again at the second part of the statement: ". . . and God divided the light from the darkness."

No way Jose! The "light" is never divided. Old Sol burns constantly. But the rotating earth puts us on the far side, away from facing the sun's energy. That energy radiates only in straight, unbending paths. When there is nothing to bend or aim it at the part of the earth turned away from it, that side has no energy to be converted into light by our air pocket. That leaves that side of the world in darkness. It is then we can see "light" refracted from other bodies in our system, like the moon. "Stars" are other suns, but they are at such remote distances from us that their "light," their energy, while also refracted by our air blanket, is only enough to make them appear at night as "twinkle, twinkle, little star." Stars are everywhere around us, but the greater proximity of our sun drowns them out when we are facing its much nearer energy.

Since the ancients who wrote the Bible were so poorly informed, their version, which we are reading verse by verse, becomes nothing more than a bogus rendition, a farce, a "prattling" of imaginary explanations for things they feared but had no understanding of.

Verse 5: "And God called the light day, and the darkness he called night. And the evening and the morning were the first day." If we consider the *real* necessities required to "create" that *First day and all they had to include, we have a beginning understanding of why I refer to the writings as Wholly Babble!* It cannot logically be considered anything else.

Verse 6: "And God said: Let there be a firmament in the midst of the waters, and let it divide the waters from the waters."

If you recall, in verse 2 we were informed that the earth was without form and void, which we've already considered as at least improbable if not impossible. But in verse 6 we see described a scene of "water, water everywhere" *with nothing* to hold it anywhere. Also in Verse 6, God is finally going to separate it, water from water, with a firmament.

Verse 7: "And God made the firmament and divided the waters which were under the firmament from the waters which were above the firmament; and it was so." If you think we are not reading fantasy then you have a very jaded opinion of what constitutes reality. Take a look at the next verse:

Verse 8: "And God called the firmament Heaven. And the evening and the morning were the second day."

Has anyone, anywhere, in all of history, ever figured out what happened to the water *above the firmament?* Verse 6 makes it clear the firmament was in the "midst" of the waters, making that above equal to that water *below* the firmament. And just how can the "heavens" be considered firm? It also indicates that "Heaven" was just then being "created," while many other verses in the Bible definitely infer that Heaven, with its army of heavenly host has always existed with God. A problem also arises over the connotative meanings of the "firmament." In today's definitions, firmament means the arch of sky above us, which we frequently call the heavens. In Biblical writing days anything referring to the "heavens" meant literally that it was "God and His Heavenly Host's" domain. But enough of the confusion over just what was being "created" on that second day. The main problem as I see it is: What happened to all that "upper" half of the water?

.... and, whilst mulling this over I suddenly knew the answer. That which remained on earth had to be "half" the water if we accept the Biblical version. Okay, so we could take one cup full out of our supply for each of the planets, moons, etc. in the Heavens, and after totally depleting earth's supply, we would not have put a cupful on even half the orbs out there. Ah . . . now we know why our scientists are having so much trouble finding traces of water on other bodies in the sky. God just didn't "create" enough of the stuff. But that is by no means all that God was short sighted on as depicted in His "Holy Word." Let's move on to:

Verse 9: "And God said: 'Let the waters under the Heavens be gathered together into one place, and let the dry land appear.' And it was so." Verse 10: "God called the dry land earth and the waters that were together He called seas. And God saw that it was good." Verse 11: "And God said: 'Let the earth put forth vegetation, plants yielding seed, and fruit trees bearing fruit in which is their seed, each according to its kind, upon the earth.' And it was so." Verse 12: "The earth brought forth vegetation, plants yielding seed according to their own kinds, and trees bearing fruit in which is their seed, each according to its kind. And God saw that it was good." Verse 13: "And there was evening and there was morning, a third day."

More than the fact that all we have read so far is highly improbable let me point out one of the Scriptures' chief weakness as recounted in the verses we've just read. Each time God "creates" something, He looks and sees that it is good. As an Omnipotent, all knowing, all Powerful God who can "create" all these things out of absolutely nothing, merely by saying: "Let there be . . .", is He maybe expecting it not to be so good, necessitating His having to do it over? Tch, tch.

Verse 14: "And God said: 'Let there be lights in the firmament of the heavens to separate the day from the night; and let them be for signs and for seasons and for days and years, (Verse 15) and let them be lights in the firmament of the heavens to give light upon the earth.' And it was so." Verse 16: "And God made the two great lights, the greater light to rule the day and the lesser light to rule the night; He made the stars also. (Verse 17) And God set them in the firmament of the heavens to give light upon the earth, (Verse 18) to rule over the day and over the night, and to separate the light from the darkness. And God saw that it was good. (Verse 19) And there was evening and there was morning, a forth day." (God had already created light and night in verses 3 & 4, the 1st day.)

1st day, 4th day? We have here the improbable claim of the separation of day and night *on the FOURTH day!* If so how were the previous three days determined? This and more of the same type problem with the scriptures was brought out by the defense in the ridiculous "Monkey Trial" in Tennessee several years ago. Bryan, a Fundamentalist expert, who lived and breathed all of the Biblical stuff with hard-core zealotry was the prosecution's chief witness. On cross examination by the defense attorney, Bryan was reduced to babbling idiocy by being shown the impossible conditions considered to be truth by the Fundamentalists.

But we must consider another extremely worrisome condition in the scriptures. We are still on the first page of the Bible and already even in these first few verses we are getting monotonous repetition of things already clearly and definitely stated. Constantly recurring repetitions are legion throughout the entire Bible, and almost as frequently, in the re-take of these scenes, "up-grades" are added to the previous version. Where these "repetitions" are depicting God's decisions and/or words, the implications are that God didn't quite say or do it right the first time over. We'll call your attention to some of the worst botches in these "retakes" as we reach them.

Verse 20: "And God said: 'Let the waters bring forth swarms of living creatures, and let birds fly above the earth across the firmament of the heavens.' (Verse 21) So God created the great sea monsters and every living creature that moves, with which the waters swarm, according to their kind, and every winged bird according to its kind. And God saw that it was good. (Verse 22) And God blessed them saying: 'Be fruitful and multiply and fill the waters in the seas, and let birds multiply on the earth.' (Verse 23) And there was evening and there was morning, a fifth day."

Immediately after "creating" all of these creatures, God gives them the order to be fruitful and multiply. None of those living creatures can be fruitful and multiply without using their own various ways of engaging in sexual mating. From this we must conclude that God was NOT opposed to fucking!

Verse 24: "And God said: 'Let the earth bring forth living creatures according to their kinds: cattle and creeping things and beasts of the earth according to their kinds.' And it was so. (Verse 25) And God made the beasts of the earth according to their kinds and the cattle according to their kinds, and everything that creeps upon the ground according to its kind. And God saw that it was good." I have trouble with the statements "..according to their kind." When and where was ". . . their kind" established? And don't forget that we are considering tens of thousands of different kinds.

Though we now could cite more improbable events and repetitions occurring since I last butted in, those flukes are minor compared to real problem with what we've just read. In the past few verses God has created all of earths many life forms including all the sea, land, and airborne creatures. *Each time He has seen that it is good.*

No mention anywhere in what we've covered is made of any living thing that is too small for mankind to see it. There is a simple answer to the problem: In the days of Biblical writing, existence of bacteria, germs, viruses, etc. was *not* even suspected, let alone describable. But a "Creator," especially one such as our Bible tries to describe, *would have known they had to be existent and ever present too.*

HAD TO BE EXISTENT TOO?

Emphatically yes! Though many such things are the causes of sickness, diseases, impairment, even fatalities, humans at least, if not all of earth's life forms, would have already become extinct if the realm of microscopic and submicroscopic life did not exist.

Dead bodies of anything, plant or animal, would not rot and disintegrate without them. The world would have become a pesthole of dead creatures that could not be gotten rid of. Our world is a gigantic terrarium and life on it can *only be maintained by a constant re-cycling of all its components.* All of that is just *one* example of the absolute necessity of micro-and-submicroscopic creatures.

It is from indisputable facts, only a few of which we have considered, that we see the first clue to just how really phony the Biblical God actually is. Witness: Not one living creature on the face of this earth can exist except by eating foodstuffs created from some other living life form. No living life form of any size or life style can exist on inorganic material only. Even grass in the fields and trees of the forests exist on rotten material made from the bodies of other once living things. However, that's the good news. As far as we know, plant life has no feelings of pain or terror, although we may be in error on that assumption. There are those who would swear that we are.

But there ARE induced horrors of pain and terror in all of the animal, marine, and fowl life that exists. Tune in on any of the wildlife shows on T.V. and see the naked fear in any creature being pursued by a stronger, faster, predatory beast. Listen to its screams, see the terror and pain when a weaker thing is chosen for lunch and is caught, torn limb from limb and eaten, many times while still alive.

An Omnipotent God, *capable* of creating this giant mill of continual carnage, suffering, slaughter, and dog eat dog necessity, would have known all of that. While "creating" it He would also have known that He was setting this carnal slaughterhouse into perpetual activation for uncounted centuries of totally sadistic treatment of its inhabitants. *And God saw this as GOOD?*

I can't, even with the most casual definition of good, apply the word to *any* of that absolutely sick worldly functioning. Yet our world full of life forms cannot, and will not, function any other way.

Oh don't forsake truth here, for some other apologetic kind of double-speak ever bubbling from the Clergy. Such a God could have absolutely NO mercy and would be incapable of loving anything he had "created" under such a diabolically hideous format. This fact alone should totally discredit any belief whatsoever in the Biblical God. But accept that as enough or refuse to even consider it. If you continue reading this book you will learn of even more ridiculous prattle and babble contained in the (Not So) Good Book.

Earlier in this book I mentioned that there are at least 14 different "Authorized" versions of the King James Version of the Bible. I goofed. I hope you will pardon me. The number 14 includes only those with almost entirely different *views* in many passages. I hope to have room in this book to quote from one Bible's "history," published as a foreword to it by the company doing the printing. To read exact "translations," as all Bible publishers claim their editions to be, then to read other versions of "sworn" to be exact translations that differ very greatly, makes one begin to wonder if he has fallen down the rabbit hole with Alice in Wonderland. But if we read just one of those versions, then compare it with one printed again a few years later by the same publishing firm, we frequently find that the exact wording in the earlier book has been changed considerably in their next editions. In researching the Bible for this book, I have inadvertently been using 3 different Bibles, all different editions from the same publishing firm, but printed over a 50 year interval. The changes in just those three Bibles during that 50 year period of their "sworn to be exact translations" is enough to make one puke because of the obvious deceptions.

But the above changes and alterations happened at only *one* company in a very short time. If you are a Religious "believer," you should now think about what has happened to the Bible over a TWO THOUSAND year interval, as it was translated from one language to another, bandied about by a multitude of different translators, editors, publishers and other un-assorted riff-raff. If a real God had "inspired" the book, it is an odds-on bet that He could no longer recognize His work in a modern day version of it. Godly protection of His Word to be sure the Bible came down to us intact, may just be one of the biggest lies the Clergy continually bleats at his congregations of today.

But let's get back to our Bible reading. Verse 26: "And God said 'Let us make man in our own image, after our likeness: and let them have dominion over the fish of the seas, and over the fowl of the air, and over the cattle, and over all the earth, and over every creeping thing that creepeth upon the earth.' Verse 27: So god created man in His own image, in the image of God created He him; male and female created He them." Verse 29: "And God said: 'Behold I have given you every herb bearing seed which is upon the face of the earth, and every tree in which is the fruit of a tree yielding seed; to you it shall be for meat.' And it was so." Verse 30: "And to every beast, and to every fowl of the air, and to everything that creepeth upon the earth where-in their is life, I have given every green herb for meat.' And it was so." Verse 31: "And God saw everything that He had made, and behold it was very good, and the evening and the morning were the sixth day." He's at it again, seeing "good" in the many centuries to come that he has just set in motion, where-in his "creations" will be subject to carnage, terror, suffering and death indescribably horrible.

Genesis 2: 1 "Thus the heavens and the earth were finished, and all the host of them." Verse 2: "And on the seventh day God ended his work which he had made and He rested on the seventh day from all of the work which He had made." Verse 3: "And God blessed the seventh day and sanctioned it because in it He had rested from all His work which God created and made." Verse 4: "These are the generations of the Heavens and of the earth when they were created in the day that the Lord God made the earth and the heavens."

We gulped all of that in one swig, without interruption, for several reasons. Reading some Biblical passages in quick small does, interrupting often to comment on that one small bit, makes our case against those verses more vividly clear. But doing the same thing on some other scenes would detract from the overall reality of gross Biblical faults and errors. Let's look at this larger bite we've just taken.

In the first place my long ago High School English teacher in San Antonio would have cringed at the incompetence evidenced by the writer of those verses. They seem to be the scribblings of a semi-literate with little understanding of anything. One of the most confusing and questionable items is in the first verse, when God says: "Let *US* make man . . ." He follows that with the statement, ". . . let *THEM* have dominion . . ." In the use of US, is God addressing the "Heavenly Host" of angels, etc.? Obviously He is referring to both male and female when He says: ". . . let THEM have . . ." for soon after the line appears that says, ". . . male and female He created them." But when we get to the next account of God's "creating" man, we will see that the creating of the female, Eve, was more like an afterthought, to correct God's oversight of Adam being lonely with no companion.

Another gross error in all of the material we have so far read is the continual confusion over the Heavens and their Hosts. Part of the time the account seems to be speaking of the arch of *visible* skies above us with the celestial orbs we can see. But at other times the same words seem to be talking about the Heavens that God and His Hosts occupy which is totally *invisible* to humanity. About the best anyone can do is *assume* which is which every time it is mentioned.

In Verse 26, we also find what will become in the next Biblical chapter, another incomprehensible self-contradiction. ". . . . and let them have dominion over the fish of the seas, and over the fowl of the air, and over the cattle, and over all the earth, and over every creeping thing that creepeth upon the earth." I do not wish to be jumping ahead of our reading, but in this case, to make our objections clear, we must. Genesis 2: 8 "And the Lord God planted a garden eastward in Eden and there He put the man he had formed." Verse 15: "And the Lord God took the man and put him into the Garden of Eden to dress it and keep it." Verse 18: "And the Lord God said, 'It is not good that the man should be alone; I will make him an help meet for him." Verse 19: (in these lines I find much to raise an eyebrow over.) "And out of the ground the Lord God formed every beast of the field, and every fowl of the air and brought them unto Adam to see what he would call them; and whatsoever Adam called every living creature, that was the name thereof." Verse 20: "And Adam gave names to all cattle, and to the fowl of the air, and to every beast of the field; but for Adam there was not found an help meet for him."

Great Grief! Objections galore rise out of all that worse than the smog in L.A.! And they produce a very similar stink. In the first Chapter of Genesis we have just read, ALL of the cattle, beasts, fowls, and etc. were "created" *before Adam was*, and in the first 6 days of God's creating. Here in the Second Chapter, they are being created because Adam has no help meet, and they are being created *after* the original 6 days of creation were completed and the 7th day in which God "rested." (Why an Omnipotent God would need rest I have no idea.) But one thing in the above lines is even more incomprehensible. Read it yourself: After all the beasts, cattle, fowl, etc. were "created," presented to Adam, and named, the line ". . . . but for Adam there was not found an help meet for him" is really silly. God is looking for a help meet for Adam from among the cattle, beasts of the field, and fowls of the air? Jeesh! Just how really incompetent can God be?

Another small objection: God has just created Adam and put him in the Garden of Eden. When, where, and in what language had Adam been taught to speak? How could he utter ANY name for any life form and understand it? And with no teaching of any language ever being mentioned by the Bible, how could Adam understand God's orders about what he could and could NOT eat from that garden? These orders are given in verse 16, well *before* the creation of Eve.

A few paragraphs back, I skipped a few Biblical verses. jumping ahead to make a point. On checking back I find that we skipped only the Biblical description of the location of Eden and the rivers that flow out of it. Since no one has ever been able to decipher any of that description and even guess at Eden's location, we may just as well omit it altogether and continue from where we are. One other point I feel is necessary. In beginning this Bible study, I was using the first Bible I mentioned. That Bible is a bit over 50 years old and has very small and non-bold lettering. Even though I am now past 80, I still read without glasses or magnification of any kind. But I *was* experiencing great problems with trying to copy from that edition. So I switched to latest version I had (published by the same company) and almost immediately discovered there had been more changes than even I had known about. Hi-ho! So what else is new? I am currently using the 1989 printing by World Publishing at Grand Rapids. If you are using *any* other Bible then it is an odds-on bet that yours will differ all the way from slightly to jarringly in many places. Just how really proficient IS God at "protecting" His word and bringing it down to us intact?

So from among all the beasts, cattle and fowl, no help meet was found for Adam, however quaint (and stupid) the search.

The "creation" of Eve is another study in unnecessary "Godly" procedures. Witness Verse 21: "And the Lord God caused a deep sleep to fall upon Adam; and he slept; and he took one of his ribs, and closed up the flesh instead thereof." (The Bible I'm using does not capitalize He when referring to God, so this time neither did I. Read it again and note the pathetic, semi-literacy of the wording and sentence structure. But there are worse things wrong with the scene: God "created" the entire Universe and the billions (to the nth power) of things in it, all out of absolutely nothing, by merely saying "Let there be . . ." He "created" all the creatures on earth, including Adam, out of dust from that earth. But when He "creates" Eve, God takes a rib out of Adam.

Knowing a few facts concerning the subjugation of women into being mere "property" for men (brought about *by the Bible*), *gives insight to the real reason this rib using modus operandi was pictured as being used by God.* Let us pause a moment for a brief recap of some of that history.

The first five books of the Bible, including Genesis, the one we are reading, is proclaimed to be the writings of Moses. They are in fact known as The Laws of Moses, which are the foundation and corner stone of Judaism. According to the Bible, Moses existed and led the Children of Israel out of slavery to the Egyptians approximately 1500 years B.C.E. There is proof galore, far too much and too involved for us to include much of here, that those first 5 books were *not* written until about 750 years B.C.E. Just one of those many proofs is the fact that the city of Ur is used for point making and supposedly sound fact in the first 5 books. The truth is that Ur did not even exist during Moses supposed life time, but *did exist and was an important city in 750 B.C.E.!* Since those first 5 books continually represent themselves as being written by Moses at least 750 years earlier, they make of themselves and the people who actually wrote them, nothing short of self aggrandizing liars. One more nail in that coffin and we'll move on: During the supposed time of Moses, approximately 1500 years B.C.E., the "children of Israel" had no means what ever of being able to read or write. Written material of any kind, in any language, would have been as useless to them as the tits on a boar hog. Approximately 750 years B.C.E. they finally adopted one of the crudest and most drastically limited means of writing ever to exist. It is known as Aramaic. By that time much of the scurvy treatment of women as mere "property" had long been well established and practiced. But regardless of the fact that women had absolutely no voice or freedom whatsoever did NOT stop some occasional very sour response and disobedience from them, their punishment for doing so not withstanding.

Even so, human nature being what it is, there was a considerable amount of hanky-panky being perpetrated by many of the men, *with some other man's "property"*. Man made rules were NOT controlling nor stopping the dilly dallying "thefts." This was causing all sorts of malcontent, rebellion, murders, and what not. The would be "controllers" amongst the Jews knew that an Omnipotent *God's* Holy orders might succeed better. So, in writing the Laws of Moses, these devious old plotters invented stories to bring the desired results about. If the first woman (and thus her descendents) came out of the first man, then she would by God's "creating" her in that manner, be a *minor and lesser* part of man, and thus be forever beholden to him.

Nailing this subjugation of women down even more craftily, they plotted the scenario of *Eve being the sucker, the "weakling," who was lured by the Serpent. Then by her tempting Adam to disobey God too, she became totally responsible for the fall of Man from Grace!* In the sequel to this book, if I ever live long enough to write it, we'll trace how this original control of women was further nailed down by "Jesus," and thus by Christianity. It is an interesting, and very informative history, the absurdity and ends of which has not only proved to be diabolically evil, but the direct cause of many of America's very serious problems right today. Truly did Shakespeare write: "Life is a tale told by an idiot, full of sound and fury and signifying nothing."

It is time now for some very important questions. If God built Eden and put within it everything that Adam needed . . . *why did He first create the Universe with its countless miles of space and the billions of objects in it. . . . and WHY did He create our whole earth? Obviously, by the Bible's own testimony, the Garden contained everything necessary for any human to ever need.* And why did He also put into that garden two things He did NOT want Adam to have? (The tree of life and the tree of the knowledge of Good and Evil.) And if God is truly all knowing and all powerful, then how come He did NOT know what would happen if He also let the Serpent into the garden? We mere men here on earth have NO Godly wisdom whatsoever, but even we know better than to leave a poisonous snake in the yard with our kids.

Adam, newly created, and a fresh rib from him turned into a "woman" signifies without question that neither of them would have any real knowledge, experience, or judgment about anything . . . especially is that so when no where in their story is it ever stated that they were ever tutored about anything. And, if God had "created" them with a built-in and adequate knowledge as part of their equipment, the Bible never even so much as hints at that either.

Quite some time ago, concerned members of some churches began to question the Biblical story of the "creation" and the fall of man from Grace along similar lines of reasoning that I have mentioned. So widespread did doubts become that the Clergy was faced with very real problems, for doubt is the beginning of and the nurturing of wisdom. Wisdom eventually rejects questionable concepts. Then quietly the "explanation" began to be heard from some of the pulpits. "The Bible's account of the Garden of Eden and the fall of man from Grace, is an allegory . . . a sort of parable . . . to explain mankind's gradual drifting away from God and becoming more and more sinful and corrupt in doing so."

The doubters were thus shushed up and the Clergy's "Holy" charade continued much as before. But our reading thus far is just the beginning of many scenes in the Bible that have continued to cause further splitting up, shattering really, of Christianity and its followers. One very large group of hard-core Christians refused absolutely and continues refusing to accept any deviation from the actual printed stories in the Bible, however ridiculous those stories are. These people are known as "Fundamentalists." Trying to penetrate their "beliefs" with reasoning or proof that they are wrong is akin to arguing with a fence post, albeit the fence post may be doing a needed service. Conversely, the Fundamentalists are destroying what little freedom and human rights we still have left in our land. That is by no means unique for *any* era of Christianity, regardless of which "cult" of it one traces the true history of.

Genesis 2: 22 "And the rib, which the Lord God had taken from the man, made He a woman, and brought her unto the man." Verse 23: "And Adam said, this is now bone of my bone, and flesh of my flesh, she shall be called woman, because she was taken out of man." Verse 24: "Therefore shall a man leave his father and his

mother, and shall cleave unto his wife; and they shall be one flesh."
Great grief! From where and when did Adam learn anything
whatsoever about any existence of a father and mother? Until the
creation of Eve he is the only human in existence. Get another jolt
for some more laughs: How did the word "wife" come into his
usage . . . not one shred of the idea or its happening had ever existed.

Still worse, God put Adam into a deep sleep for the procedure.
Whence cometh his knowledge or understanding that she was bone
of his bone and flesh of his flesh?

If we consider all of that reasonably, it further proves that all of
the whole yarn was written only after centuries of time had indelibly
stamped those customs and practices into the Jewish race. To them,
things they were accustomed to would help convince them that
indeed the writings were from God, because He was telling them
what they already believed. After gaining that foothold, *then the
would be "controllers" could dictate "God's" orders to suit themselves.*
There is an almost unlimited amount of proof that that *was* the
way and the method by which "God" was created!

If your credulity was not ruptured by our readings thus far,
Verse 25 should jar it up like a major earthquake, for there the
scriptures become even sillier:

Verse 25: "They were both naked and not ashamed." Neither
of them knew anything about clothing or sex, nor any Godly orders
against it, so why should their being unashamed be necessary to
even mention? They could hardly have any feeling or opinions
about the matter at all.

But if we keep remembering that all of this was actually written
centuries later than it was said to have been written it is less trouble
to pick it to pieces. Remember also that for centuries before written
Biblical edicts came into existence, Jewish regards for each other
and the regards for tribal laws were NOT effective in stopping
sexual dalliance with other men's "property." Throughout the "Laws
of Moses" then, any sexuality out of "wedlock" *had* to be shown as
an affront to and a sin against God and God's will, not just against
man made rules. Even today people in all walks of life constantly

and continually break all sorts of man-made "rules" right here in America.

A man's jealousy over any woman he claimed as his own, whether wife or daughter, and the total "horror" of her possibly conceiving a child from another man was just probably the most trouble making condition that existed among the Jews in those days. Throughout traceable history identical conditions of sexual problems have *always* plagued all races controlled by Deity Religions. Conversely those sexual problems *never* arose nor were of any concern to races that were not warped and tainted by belief in Gods and their Godly "laws" concerning sex and morality. That fact alone should raise great doubts about much of Christian (so called) "morality."

Genesis 3: 1 "Now the serpent was more subtil (biblical spelling) than any beast of the field which the Lord God had made. And he said unto the woman "Yea, hath God said, Ye shall not eat of every tree of the garden?" Verse 2 "And the woman said unto the serpent, We may eat of the fruit of the trees of the garden." Verse 3 "But of the fruit of the tree in the midst of the garden, God hath said Ye shall not eat of it, neither shall ye touch it, lest ye die."

There are remarkable circumstances in all of that. The serpent, a beast of the field, has not only the ability to talk to humans, but to con them. And here in the space of a couple of none explanatory verses, Eve has become fully versed in conversation and knows of the warning concerning the famed tree and its forbidden fruit. The probability of any of that being true is flippantly, carelessly left up to the reader as if all of it is indisputable. Another glaring fault is this: When all of this was actually written, Satan had not yet been fully invented. His future image was barely beginning to emerge allegorically. But over the years the "serpent" in the Garden tale has generally been identified as a snake. He is much more emphatically identified by the Clergy now as the devil in disguise. Obviously the enmity between snakes and humans had already been firmly established when the Garden story was written.

Verse 4: "And the serpent said unto the woman 'Ye shall not

surely die. Verse 5: "For God doth know that in the day ye eat thereof, then your eyes shall be opened and ye shall be as gods, knowing good and evil. Verse 6 "And when the woman saw that the tree was good for food and that it was pleasant to the eyes, and a tree to be desired to make one wise, she took of the fruit thereof and did eat, and gave also to her husband with her and he did eat. Verse 7: "And the eyes of both of them were opened and they knew they were naked; and they sewed fig leaves together and made themselves aprons."

A very great deal of illogical whimsy appears in verse 5 above. First, God is (perhaps accidentally) portrayed as being jealous should a human become aware of a knowledge that apparently the entire Heavenly Host knows. This will be nailed down as a certainty when we reach verse 22. There is another questionable thing gleaming like an unintentional revelation in verse 6: ". . . the tree was good for food . . . pleasant to the eyes . . . and a tree to be desired to make one wise . . ." but this "creator" God has ordained that the fruit of that tree (which will acquaint one with the knowledge of good and evil) is forbidden to humans. Why would He forbid usable knowledge of any kind to his own "children?" My meaning here will be more obvious and logical when we reach verse 22.

Verse 8 "And they heard the voice of the Lord God walking in the garden in the cool of the day; (maybe God sunburns easily) and Adam and his wife hid themselves from the presence of the Lord God amongst the trees of the garden." Verse 9 "And the Lord God called unto Adam and said unto him, Where art thou?" Verse 10 "And he said I heard thy voice in the garden, and I was afraid because I was naked, and I hid myself." (One thing is for sure: When the writers of the first five books of the Bible were finished, there were no "Ands" left any where around. They'd used them all up.) Verse 10 is another example of illogical accounting. God created both Adam and Eve as naked as jaybirds, and has continually dealt with them in their nude state since. Then after eating of the tree of the knowledge of "good and evil," not only is

Adam ashamed of his nudity, He hides from God who made him that way. Obviously none of that will hold water. It is then an attempt to make nudity a depraved condition when actually it is no such thing at all. Bible writers who continued this theme in later books in the Bible finally were presenting nudity as an absolute abomination in God's abhorrence of it. That too was a process of evolving a warped idea into great psychological prominence that was illogical and meaningless to begin with. In America that absurdity has resulted in all sorts of laws concerning "indecent exposure" as well as many very crass and uptight opinions about it.

Verse 11: "And he said Who told thee thou wast naked? Hast thou eaten of the tree whereof I commanded thee that thou shouldest not eat?" Verse 12: "And the man said The woman whom that givest to be with me, she gave me of the tree and I did eat." Verse 13: "And the Lord God said unto the woman What is this thou hast done? And the woman said The serpent beguiled me and I did eat."

There is a point in those few verses that needs to be shouted from the roof tops. When asked a point blank question concerning his actions, Adam tries ducking responsibility and blaming the woman. When the woman is asked about her deed, she passes blame to the serpent. This has been a growing tendency of our populace for some time, a condition that was not in widespread usage before WW II. Oh yes, there was a considerable amount of buck passing then too, but NOT in the epidemic deluge that it has come to be in the America of now. Today NO ONE will assume responsibility for anything that he can possibly blame on some one else or on some condition beyond his control. NO ONE is at personal fault about anything. Passing the buck has become a way of life, and mass refusal to accept responsibility, just blame some one else, has become our credo. The results of this swarming sea of irresponsibility, wind up more and more frequently in our already over crowded and far behind court systems, further jamming and confounding an already warped and out of balance branch of our

government. Men whose word was their bond, and/or faced-up to
their own actions and decisions, have almost become an extinct
species.

Verse 14: "And the Lord God said unto the serpent Because
thou hast done this thou art cursed above all cattle and above
every beast of the field; upon thy belly shalt thou go, and dust
shalt thy eat all the days of thy life." Verse 15: "And I will put
enmity between thee and the woman, and between thy seed and
her seed; it shall bruise thy head, and thou shalt bruise his heel."
Verse 16: "Unto the woman he said, I will greatly multiply thy
sorrow and thy conception; in sorrow thou shalt bring forth
children, and thy desire shalt be to thy husband, and he shall rule
over thee." Verse 17: "And unto Adam he said, Because thou hast
harkened unto the voice of thy wife and hast eaten of the tree of
which I commanded thee, saying, Thou shalt not eat of it; cursed
is the ground for thy sake; in sorrow shalt thou eat of it all the days
of thy life;" Verse 18: "Thorns also and thistles shalt it bring forth
to thee, and thou shalt eat the herb of the field; Verse 19: "In the
sweat of thy face shalt thou eat bread, till thou return into the
ground, for out of it wast thou taken; for dust thou art, and unto
dust shalt thou return."

Verse 16 above has been a millstone around the neck of women
in all races influenced by this ancient yarn, for all of the centuries
since it was first dreamed up by crotchety old monks. As we have
previously noted, that long ago era was when they were putting
together the initial Aramaic writings that recanted scores of folk
lore tales that had been told around the campfires at night for
centuries. I believe it worth repeating: Hundreds of the story-tellers
aged, died, then were replaced with new blood. The yarns frequently
differed from camp to camp. Some camps had stories others had
not heard. Many of the yarns had been taken from other races and
other "beliefs." All of these various tales were gradually giving
credence to, and inventing a God as their source and instigator.
Those idealistic Gods had most frequently evolved from still more
ancient tales of super-human influences on people. So,

approximately 750 years B.C.E. this hodge-podge of superstitious nonsense was finally being written. Thus Verse 16, a mere sliver of the farcical whole, has resulted in many centuries of unchangeable belief that women were *supposed* to suffer in childbirth. Further, all of it has led to centuries of dominance over women by men, often times with inexcusably brutish and sadist cruelty. Even when physical violence is absent, women are, even to this day in America, still treated as incapable and undeserving of equal recognition and treatment. In addition, with the Bible clearly and unmistakably convicting the first woman of being the cause of the fall of man from Grace, most men consider women an easy mark for clandestine sexual excursions. Unfortunately for the ladies, the New Testament not only endorses this put down on women woefully detailed and insisted on by the Old Testament's first five books, but actually enhances and multiplies the pressure . . . all in the name of Christ. No woman alive today will live long enough to see much change in these very harmful "mind-sets" that have mesmerized mankind, and dictated his actions and decisions for centuries. Since our Society has reeked with this addled nonsense for so long, the stench has penetrated countless men who've never gone to church or read the Bible at all. It is somewhat like planting gourds, citrons, watermelons, cantaloupes, and cucumbers all in close proximity to each other. None of the different types of vines planted in that manner will produce anything usable or desirable.

Verse 20: "And Adam called his wife's name Eve; because she was the mother of all living." Verse 21: "Unto Adam also and to his wife did the Lord God make coats of skins, and clothed them."

Throughout our reading thus far, another ridiculous thing is being firmly planted in each succeeding generation's thinking and practices. Adam and his "woman" were "created" naked and began living their lives in that manner. Neither was ashamed for being that way. The excuse given for that is that they *didn't know they were naked!* Unfortunately the same verses never mention God's appearance nor whether He was "clothed" or not . . . but even more pointedly: What in heck would He have been clothed in?

Ah . . . but after eating of the forbidden fruit, the two ARE *ashamed*, to the point of covering themselves with an "apron" made from fig leaves. A nude person can only use an "apron" to cover his/ her genitalia. Whence cometh their shame of genitalia? It was only one part, in fact the smallest part of their nudity.

To plant the idea forever firmly in all God believers thereafter, the Bible states that God Himself then makes them garments from skins. We will return to that non sequitur in a few moments.

In those verses then, is the totally wrong concept implanted forever in Biblical adherent's minds that nudity is obscene and vulgar. Few if any are the beliefs created by the Bible that are more patently ridiculous. But we will consider the arguments on that at another time. There are far too many idiotic concepts in the "Scriptures" for us to waste a great amount of time and space on one point, however wrong and troublesome it has become.

Ridiculously, the scene of God making those garments has resulted in gross indignation about the human body unless completely clothed by gargantuan audiences for centuries, all the while the same scene was totally ignored by another large group of fanatical bigots that became violently active just in the past few decades. This group began a protest movement against using animal skins and furs for clothing. While being a faction of environmental protection groups, they were usually members of the anti-cruelty to animals society. As with nearly all such endeavors their ranks became riddled with extremists. For a while, a woman wearing a fur coat was grossly in danger of having acid thrown in her face. Others experienced thrown globs of feces, rotten eggs, paint . . . or anything disgusting and ruinous to herself and her garb. In these examples of fanatic *non-thinking* is one very pertinent point that has occurred continually over the centuries. It is well worth considering:

A few short verses of one scene in the Bible became a "moral" command for countless people for thousands of years, i.e., that nudity is vulgar and obscene. While equal stress on another part of the same scene, i.e., God Himself using animal skins to make clothing is thereafter totally ignored by the same herds. There are countless similarly idiotic examples throughout the Bible with identical opposing results as just described developing from them. As the wind blows, so go the fallen leaves. But when the wind changes, the leaves change their direction with no thought whatsoever. So like those leaves are the brain-dead *Religionists! Unthinking fanatics all, just different in the degree of their affliction!*

Verse 22: "And the Lord God said; Behold, the man is become as one of us, to know good and evil; and now, lest he put forth his hand and take also of the tree of life, and eat, and live forever:" Verse 23: "Therefore the Lord God sent him forth from the Garden of Eden to till the ground from whence he was taken." Verse 24: "So he drove out the man, and he placed at the east of the garden of Eden Cherubims, and a flaming sword which turned every way, to keep the way of the tree of Life."

In those three verses are great weaknesses that should have caused any literate person to balk at believing. In verse 22 God is apparently speaking to the Heavenly Host when he says: ". . . is become as one of us." There are so many different meanings possible in those words that it is hard to know where to begin. This is the second time that God's remarks have been directed at his "Host" of Heavenly beings. But also, once again, God's intentions towards Adam clearly show un-Godly like partiality. He creates an entire Universe, our own Solar system, our world and its thousands of various life-forms, plus the Garden of Eden replete with everything the man can use, even putting the tree of knowledge plus the tree of life in it, creates a help meet for Adam . . . then *forbids him knowledge and eternal life, both of which His "Heavenly Host" have in totality!* Take all of that in any context whatsoever and it not only shows *partiality*, but also, *discrimination!* Those two weak minded and erroneous mind-sets are devastatingly unfair and cruel regardless of whom their owner is. In addition to all of the trouble and heartaches they cause for the victims, they also lower their practitioner to the level of childish and incompetent judgment. Worse still, would an Omnipotent, All Loving God be foolish enough to place them right in easy reach of a mere "baby" as far as experience and dependability of right decisions is concerned, especially if the "baby" was NOT to taste them? Then would he put in that "baby-bed" a wily Serpent? Worse still, AFTER the first tree is eaten from, God again shows more jealousy and favoritism by hastening to drive the pair out of the Garden lest they eat of the other tree and live forever, as the Heavenly Host does. For there was God's statement: ". . . is become as one of US!"

But now look at something that occurs in many places in the Bible. Read verse 22 again and you will note that the end of it is chopped off, the sentence NOT complete. As I stated, this chopping off occurs in several places in the Bible, but never is there any explanation or excuse. Godly "protecting" of his Word again I suppose. Reading it as it is written leaves me the opinion that a very great deal more of it needs to be chopped off.

Genesis 4: 1 "And Adam knew Eve his wife, and she conceived, and bare Cain, and said, I have gotten a man from the Lord." This verse gives a very good example of how wrong interpretations become "mind-sets" that pass along and perpetuate wrong ideas from the wrong places.

Through-out the Christian millions, for all of the years I can remember, there has been a predominantly general feeling that the "original" sin was one of sex between Adam and Eve: thus it has become firmly anchored into countless minds that *fucking* WAS the original sin therefore IS the worst of evils and a guaranteed ticket to hell. I have heard sermons by preachers who seemed to have that conviction themselves. Since that can easily be disproved by the Bible's verses, the wrong opinions about it that infest much of our populace has to be because sex, nudity, etc., per se, has become such a forbidden subject and practice, that these brain-washed people are seeing "sin-spooks" where none exist. It is part and parcel of the mania against kids knowing anything about sex whatsoever.

What a pity!

Verse 2: "And she again bare his brother Abel. And Abel was a keeper of sheep, but Cain was a tiller of the ground." Verse 3: "And in process of time it came to pass, that Cain brought of the fruit of the ground an offering unto the Lord." Verse 4: "Abel, he also brought of the firstlings of his flock and of the fat thereof. And the Lord had respect unto Abel and to his offering." Verse 5: "But unto Cain and to his offering he had not respect. And Cain was very wroth and his countenance fell." Verse 6: "And the Lord said unto Cain, Why art thou wroth, and why is thy countenance fallen?" Verse 7: "If thou doest well, shalt thou not be accepted? And if thou doest not well, sin lieth at the door. And unto thee shall be his desire and thou shalt rule over him." Verse 8: "And Cain talked with his brother Abel; and it came to pass, when they were in the field, that Cain rose up against Abel his brother, and slew him." Verse 9: "And the Lord said unto Cain: Where is Abel thy brother? And he said, I know not: Am I my brother's keeper?" Verse 10: "And he said, What hast thou done? the voice of thy brother's blood calleth to me from the ground." Verse 11: "And now art thou cursed from the earth, which has opened her mouth to receive thy brother's blood from thy hand." Verse 12: "When thou tillest the ground, it shall not henceforth yield unto thee her strength, a fugitive and vagabond shalt thou be in the earth."

Few writings, supposedly written as truth, are as clearly without logical basis as those verses just cited. God ordered man out of Eden; that he *till the earth for sustenance, getting it only by the sweat of his brow, while plagued with thorns and thistles and reluctant earth an added worry.* Then Cain, having labored in that manner, brings of the first fruits of his labors an offering to God, and is the first to bring an offering. But God respects this NOT! On the other hand, shepherds have NOT that much really hard labor to raise flocks. Abel brings some of his herd's young, and God DOES respect that. Here again, for no logical reason whatsoever, is God displaying infantile and harmful discrimination and prejudices. Then He has the gall to ask why His illogical put down of Cain makes the man mad and dejected. He then adds insult to injury by telling Cain that if he does well he WILL be respected? How has Cain not done well? No logical explanation; merely a quip about sin being at Cain's door. When? How? Not one word of Biblical explanation is even mentioned. If the Bible is carefully read entirely, these kinds of mystical abstractions pop up again and again. Surely a very dull intellect is required to read such poorly written, pointless text and give credence to it. Indeed such people apparently *do have* the "faith" of a little child.

The immediate reaction of a man slapped unfairly is to slap back. Enraged, Cain slays Abel, and of course this is decidedly wrong. But wasn't anger stirred up by the unreasonable actions of God? Similar and even more vivid examples of God's total unfairness abound throughout the Old Testament. The biggest mystery to me is how and why clergy and flocks of this alleged Deity have so thoroughly ignored them all, and continue to believe in such an ungodly being; especially while clinging to the obvious myth of Him being a God of Love, Compassion, and forgiveness.

Verse 13: "And Cain said unto the Lord, My punishment is greater than I can bear." Verse 14: "Behold, thou hast driven me out this day from the face of the earth, and from thy face shall I be hid; and I shall be a fugitive and vagabond in the earth, and it shall come to pass that everyone that findeth me shall slay me." Verse 15: "And the Lord said unto him, Therefore whosoever slayeth Cain, vengeance shall be taken on him sevenfold. And the Lord set a mark upon Cain, lest any finding him should kill him." Verse 16: "And Cain went out from the presence of the Lord and dwelt in the Land of Nod on the east of Eden."

When I was a kid in Texas I knew many people who, in the unreasonable prejudices of the day against the Negro race, believed that black skin was the "Mark of Cain," spoken of in that 15th verse. That seemed to be the general assumption all over the south, and was just very probably at least ONE of the excuses for the hatred. Obviously, any and all who subscribed to such perjured testimony were incapable of thinking. Even if black skin HAD been the "Mark of Cain," how did it survive through the flood where in everyone perished except Noah and his immediate family?

I can't keep from smiling at another idiom from those quaint days. When some question about a child's parentage cropped up amongst the gossips, some old crone, looking archly "informed" would smirk: "There must have been a nigger in the woodpile." Noah must have had quite a woodpile to build the ark. Soo . . . maybe black skin IS the mark of Cain after all. Anyhow if so, a heck of a lot of people are going to have to suffer "seven-fold" vengeance . . . especially a lot of folks down south. And by the way, just what would be sevenfold Hell, hungh?

Starting at the place we quit reading, Genesis 4: 15, there follows many verses tracing the supposed progeny of Cain and of Adam. All of these descendents are supposedly the beginning of the human race, therefore we MUST note that during that early era, *no method of writing had even been thought of, let alone actually conceived and accomplished!* Despite that, beginning with Genesis 4: 16, there are dozens of generations reported stemming from both Adam and Cain. Worse, all of these questionable and doubtful lineages would have had to cover many centuries, for the average ages of the males listed as a continuing part of the family line, are stated to be in the hundreds of years, *and them still begetting both sons and daughters.* Put all of that together and there is no way to even assume that those family tracings could in any manner whatsoever be credible. Even with all of the technology and written records of the past few centuries, no one alive today could accurately trace his actual family line back more than a century or two . . . from there back it would strictly be speculation and random guessing. So in an era when there was NO methods of writing, no documents, and no records . . . the hundreds of years reported as *facts of those lineages can only be, sheer nonsense!*

For these reasons, we'll skip all that prattle and begin again where that incredible list gets us down to Noah. To introduce the fairy tale about Noah, let's begin with Genesis 6: 5 "And God saw that the wickedness of man was great in the earth, and that every imagination of the thoughts of his heart was only evil continually."

Now wait just a doggone minute! If you have carefully read

the verses as we have come forward, right from the very first word
of the Scriptures, *not one single line has ever been given to the humans
that are involved, as to WHAT WAS WICKED OR GOOD!* The
Commandments of God will NOT be given for many centuries
yet, and with NO word from God to those rapidly multiplying
people as to what WAS good, and what WAS evil, *how were they
supposed to know how NOT to conduct themselves?* But there
immediately follows something even more unlikely. Witness:

Genesis 6: 6 "And it repented the Lord that he had made man
on earth; and it grieved him at his heart." Though there are more
than 19,000 outright flukes, provable errors, and self contradictions
in the Bible, that brief line may very well be one of the worst! Just
consider: We are time and time again, endlessly told of God's
Supremacy, his ultimate ability, power, and understanding. Time
and again we are shown that this ultra Supreme Being tolerates
NO even small mistake from any of His "creations." Could such a
Being *really* plan and instigate something that would be *HIS* fault
for making an irredeemable mistake? Also, doing something that
turns out badly enough to "Grieve" one in his heart, is a *human*
type failing and emotion. Certainly it is NOT a credible thing for
an Omnipotent God. The next verse shows God as having an even
worse fault.

Verse 7: "And the Lord said, I will destroy man whom I have
created from the face of the earth; both man and beast, and the
creeping thing, and the fowls of the air, for it repenteth me that I
have made them." Verse 8: "But Noah found grace in the eyes of
the Lord."

When a mere man creates something that doesn't work to suit
him, he first tries to determine where the fault lies. Then he goes
back to the drawing board and conceives ways to *correct the machine
so that it will work satisfactorily. A Supreme God can only get pissed off
and DESTROY it? And while He is at it, is going to destroy scads of
harmless other creatures who have NO guilt what ever? And these same
creatures who have no fault were seen by Him as GOOD when he gave
life to them?* Anyway we consider this, it pictures God as being

psychotic and having an emotional disaster area in His belfry rather than, and instead of, a mind.

Verse 8: "But Noah found grace in the eyes of the Lord." Verse 9: "These are the generations of Noah: Noah was a just man and perfect in his generations, and Noah walked with God." Nowhere in the verses we skipped, nor in all of those dozens of generations descending from Adam or Cain, is any mention made of who is making Noah's generations *good*, nor what they were doing or not doing to achieve it. Despite all the lack of explanation as to *why*, we now find that Noah can still walk and talk with God. In verses 10, 11, and 12 we find once again some totally unnecessary repetition of things already detailed out in previous verses, so I omit them. Verse 13: "And God said unto Noah, The end of all flesh is come before me, for the earth is filled with violence through them; and behold, I will destroy them with the earth." Verse 14: "Make thee an ark of gopher wood . . ." There is no point in detailing out all of the measurements and instructions concerning this ark. However, two of those requirements are of importance for our purposes here. Verse 16: "A window shalt thou make to the ark . . . and the door of the ark shalt thou set in the side . . ." Please keep in mind that the one window and one door are the only openings in the ark.

Ask almost any regular Church member about the number of animals, birds, etc. that were to be allowed on the ark and they will promptly say "Two of everything." I don't really credit these types with having enough knowledge or wits to even have an opinion about anything concerning God or Religion. For any thinking individual who can read the Bible as it is now revised and revised and revised, his usual conclusion will likely be that the Bible is its own worst enemy. It disproves its validity so often and repeatedly that I have considerable difficulty understanding how and why it has had, and even worse, still has, such tremendous impact on supposedly *intelligent* people of today.

Verse 19: "And of every living thing of all flesh, two of every sort shalt thou bring into the ark, to keep them alive with thee;

they shall be male and female." Now that seems to verify that most Church member's idea about there being two of everything was correct. But once again, the writers of the Bible do a retake and change the script.

Verse 21: "And take unto thee of all food that is eaten; and thou shalt gather it to thee and it shall be for food for thee and for them." Verse 22: "Thus did Noah according to all that God commanded him, so did he." (The instructions in Verse 21 will presently be shown as of very great importance.)

Genesis 7: 1 "And the Lord said unto Noah, Come thou and all thy house into the ark; for thee I have seen righteous before me in this generation." Verse 2: "Of every clean beast thou shalt take to thee by sevens, the male and his female; and of beasts that are not clean by two, the male and his female." Verse 3: "Of fowls also of the air by sevens, the male and the female; to keep seed alive on the face of the earth." Verse 4: "For yet seven days, and I will cause it to rain upon the earth forty days and forty nights; and every living substance that I have made will I destroy off the face of the earth." Verse 5: "And Noah did according unto all that the Lord had commanded him."

You will note that the script indeed has been changed and that the generally accepted yarn of *two of every kind* has been altered from the original instructions. This increase would mean thousands *more* beasts and birds than we were first informed of. Still another problem here is the fact that most types of beasts and birds do not inhabit *every* continent, and frequently, only certain locales on one continent. How indeed could Noah have complied with God's orders then? And in just *seven days?*

A moment ago I asked you to remember the instructions in Verse 21 above. So now look at the problem with it: Many fowls of the air, and even many more of the beasts that must be included in the ark, *are carnivorous only!* There are NO indications that God is going to change or interfere with regular diets or functions of living while these creatures are on the ark. When we get to the *total time* they will be on that ark, this food problem as well as an additional problem I will point out, puts the whole story into the realm of very poorly written fantasy fiction, where-in all of reality is by-passed and put to naught for the sole purpose of telling the yarn. Let's look at another problem before we continue: If we remember that the tale of Noah is many, many years before Abraham, and thus centuries before the destruction of Sodom and Gomorrah, we can only place Noah and the flood many, many years before the iron age, in other words during an era *when tools did NOT consist of much more than crude clubs acquired from easily picked up parts of fallen trees. Certainly pitch, which God required the ark to be water-proofed with, had NOT been invented, nor had anything like an efficient axe been dreamed of. How in heck could Noah have cut and fashioned all that Herculean amount of Gopher wood and with what could he have nailed it together?*

Verse 6: "And Noah was six hundred years old when the flood of waters was upon the earth." This is still a lesser age than the main persons of Biblical lineage before Noah, many of which were stated to be two or three hundred years older than this when they were *still* begetting sons and daughters. Scientists who have diligently delved into that era have proved beyond any reasonable doubt that those early human inhabitants of earth seldom lived more than 30 to 40 years of age. But what are facts to a person hooked on "faith" in God's word?

Verse 7: "And Noah went in, and his sons, and his wife, and his sons wives with him, into the ark, because of the waters of the flood." Verse 8: "Of clean beasts, and of beasts that are not clean, and of fowls, and of everything that creepeth on the earth," Verse 9: "There went in two and two unto Noah into the ark, the male and the female, as God had commanded Noah." The writer of these verses forgot that clean beasts and all the fowls were to be by sevens. It is no wonder that readers rarely get it right either.

Verse 10: "And it came to pass after seven days that the waters of the flood were upon the earth." Verse 11: "In the six hundredth year of Noah's life, in the second month, the seventh day of the month, the same day were all the fountains of the great deep broken up, and the windows of heaven were opened." Verse 12: "And the rain was upon the earth forty days and forty nights." If we recall 7: 4, God gave his final orders of loading the ark just 7 days before start of the flood, and in 7: 5, Noah did all that God commanded him to do. WOW! Not even considering the many creatures that would be loaded by sevens, but just considering the whole menagerie by its multitude of twos, seven days is an inconceivably short time for all that to be accomplished, even if all of the food stuff needed had already been acquired and loaded. And what of the beasts and birds not even dwelling in that area? But worse strains on our credulity are fast approaching.

The next few verses are again a rehash, a retelling of what we have just been told in the past few verses, so there is no point in our repeating them. In this particular re-hash, no drastic changes over the first telling of it are apparent, with the one exception that the animals and fowls that are to be loaded by sevens apparently has been forgotten by the writer. I have never seen a reasonable explanation as to why the writers of the Bible continually re-wrote what they had already detailed out completely. There are exceptions. First telling of a particular yarn frequently portrays things happening that God seems unaware of. In retelling of the same yarn the second version corrects that. Why they then did not delete the erroneous version is anybody's guess.

Verses 17 through 22 tell of the rising of the flood, bearing up of the ark, and all living substances and creatures of the earth being destroyed. Another problem stares us in the face with that description: Every living substance is destroyed. Now a seed is a living thing, even if not developed any further that its seed stage. God has not told Noah to load any seeds nor any sprouts, plant settings or any other means of saving any of earth's vegetation or foliage . . . no flora, only fauna. Presently, as we see the flood ending and the waters receding, another provable error in God's word will become overtly blatant and undeniable.

From verses 17 through 23 we are told of the waters covering even the mountains and wiping out all life everywhere. But verse

24 is a shocker for those remembering only the "forty days and forty nights" of rainfall, especially if they consider that as the *flood!* "And the waters prevailed upon earth an hundred and fifty days." Hey! This is in addition to the 40 days and nights of the rain! But we are still nowhere near to the end of confinement for those on the ark. We'll get back to the total time after we examine another Biblical oversight.

Let us consider just ONE animal. I spent a good many years raising this type animal commercially and know considerably more about its problems than most people ever think of as being a problem. The lowly Pig is our example! One 5 month old pig, roughly equal in development to a teenaged human, to be productive and healthy, requires six pounds of high potency, high protein-content feed per day. She also needs gallons of fresh, clean water. This daily intake results in adding one pound of flesh to the pig, five pounds of pig shit she must excrete, along with more than a gallon of urine. Five pounds of pig shit and more than a gallon of urine every day, rain or shine, from ONE young animal! Various animals have similar intakes and disposal habits, some of them less amounts, some as much or even more. But ALL living creatures do it . . . yeah hon, including Noah, his three sons, and all of each one's wives, a total of eight humans on the ark and thousands of beasts and fowls of all kinds. For a real good look at that let's go back to Genesis 7: 16; "And they went in . . . . and the Lord shut him in!" In some versions of the Bible, the exact words are ". . . and the Lord sealed them in." Remember that I asked you not forget that the ark had only ONE door, and ONE window. There are no other openings ever mentioned, and in short, NO DISPOSAL SYSTEM! And God never mentioned any such in His instructions of how to build the ark. In that closed-in ark, the amount of feces and urine that would be excreted would be over the animal's heads in a very short time, and the odor and gaseous fumes from all of that would be lethal to the animals themselves, let alone the humans. Obviously there is much wrong with God's Word on the story of the flood and the ark. This is only one example of over 19,000 similar patently ridiculous goofs in the Holy Bible. Is there really any wonder why I call it the Wholly Babble?

Genesis 8: 1; "And God remembered Noah, and every living thing, and all the cattle that were with him in the ark; and God made a wind to pass over the earth, and the waters asswaged." (Biblical spelling) (Verses 2 and 3 are similar backing off of the flood.) Verse 4: "And the ark rested in the seventh month, on the seventeenth day of the month, upon the mountains of Ararat." (Remarkable! Especially since this era is centuries before any method of writing had been invented, let alone any way to measure, or identify months, days, or years!) But we are still not anywhere near the end of all the creatures being incarcerated on the ark . . . still with no disposal system.

Verse 5: "And the waters decreased continually until the tenth month; in the tenth month, on the first day of the month, were the tops of the mountains seen." From the seventh month (verse 4) until the tenth month in verse 5, we're shown another big lapse of time that there is still no place to unload the ark. Only the tops of the mountains are clear of water. If we count back, adding all the incarcerated time together, we are being told that men, women, beasts, fowls, and all the creepy, crawly things in nature have been sealed up in that boat for over six months . . . and there will be considerable time yet before they can be let out. The one young pig I told you about, in the same length of time, would have needed nearly a ton of feed, many gallons of clean water, and as a result would have excreted well over half a ton of pig shit and nearly 300 gallons of urine. Okay, and if she had a male with her all those amounts would be doubled. Now multiply the food needs as well as the resulting excretions of thousands of *pairs* of critters of all sizes and kinds, plus eight adult humans, and tell me how the story of the "flood" with Noah's ark can possibly be credible. Yet, it is a part of *God's Holy Word!*

Okay, the ark has come to rest near the top of a mountain. Genesis 8: 6; "And it came to pass, at the end of forty days, that Noah opened the window of the ark which he had made." Verse 7:

"And he sent forth a raven which went forth to and fro, until the waters were dried up from off the earth." Verse 8: "Also he sent forth a dove from him, to see if the waters were abated from off the face of the ground." Verse 9" "But the dove found no rest for the sole of her foot; and she returned to him into the ark; for the waters were on the face of the whole earth; then he put forth his hand, and took her, and pulled her in unto him into the ark." Verse 10: "And he stayed yet another seven days, and again he sent forth the dove out of the ark." Verse 11: "And the dove came into him in the evening, and lo, in her mouth was an olive leaf pluckt (Biblical spelling) off. So Noah knew that the waters were abated from off the earth." A few paragraphs back I told you we'd shortly find another big Biblical blooper, and there it is. God, in numerous verses we've scanned has sworn to destroy every living thing on earth; in fact he has sworn to destroy everything He hast made. Yea, verily! And here, with the destruction now complete and its killing tool the flood just receding, the dove brings back a freshly plucked olive leaf!

Verse 12: "And he stayed yet another seven days (boy, is incarcerated time on the ark piling up!) and sent forth the dove which returned not again unto him any more."

Verse 13: "And it came to pass in the six hundredth and first year; in the seventh month, the first day of the month, the waters were dried up from off the earth; and Noah removed the covering of the ark, and looked, and behold, the face of the ground was dry." Verse 14: "And in the second month, on the seventh and twentieth day of the month; was the earth dried." (You can take your choice here. V. 13 says it was dry the first day of the seventh month and V. 14 disputes that by saying it was dry on the 27th day of the second month. Is that another flub-dub or is the second telling of it taking place in the following year? Either way nothing but the raven and the dove have been released so you should also remember that "stuff" in the sealed up ark had to be getting mighty deep in there. In fact it is almost as deep as the "stuff" we are reading in the Bible.)

I resolved a long time ago to keep the size of this book, as near as possible, limited to the usual thickness of most books that people will buy and read. Non-fiction books are not usually very fast sellers even when they are not extra thick. That decision dictated that I limit this book to approximately 60 to 65,000 words. That is less than a third of the words needed to discuss just a very small fraction of Biblical nonsense.

Tearing down just the most obvious and glaring nonsense in the Bible, with out even considering the minor glitches, would require several books of this size. I hope to live long enough to finish the second book in that very much needed published works list. I am considering *Planet of the Gods* as its title. For those of you who are still with me, there will be two main topics in that book. (1.) Today there is great pressure on our Congress and Federal courts to make it mandatory that the Ten Commandments be posted in all Government buildings and in all public schools. Thus our first task in *Planet of the Gods* will be to take a careful look at Moses and the whole scene when he gets those commandments from God on top of old smoky. You've been mislead and misinformed by the Clergy and the movies on that subject. When we take a look at what the Bible *really* says about it, and how desperately wrong are the agitators who are demanding laws to post it all over our land, you just might get a very real shock.

And (2.) Millions of people nation wide are totally hooked on being "saved" from eternal Hell by the "sacrifice" of Jesus on the cross. I propose to not only show you, but also *to PROVE to you, that the whole thing is a colossal hoax! It is the bloodiest, most costly, and certainly the cruelest hoax ever perpetrated on humanity!*

And you need have no fear whatsoever in learning the truth. You will NOT spend an eternity in hell, no matter what you do or don't do on this earth during your entire life time . . . which is all too short to begin with, let alone allowing it to be hamstrung and stripped of all the best pleasures and rewards of it, by a bunch of bigotry and superstitious nonsense.

So please come with me to the *Planet of The Gods* and see for yourself just how much, and in how many ways, you are being cheated every day of your life. It certainly cannot harm you to find out. And I do appreciate very much, your buying this book. In future years you may eventually decide that it was the best buy you ever made.

Thank you, and Namaste, Jack

BIBLIOGRAPHY

(Partial list in no Special order)

The Holy Bible. Choose any version you like; there are many different ones with multiple variations galore.

THE JUDAEO-CHRISTIAN BIBLE FULLY TRANSLATED

Volumes one through seven, written by William Harwood, Ph.D. 1935-Published by and available from *www.Imprintbooks.com* in the United States.

AGE OF REASON

Thomas Paine. Wet Water Publications. RR 1 Box 62 Rushville, PA 18839

THE ENCYCLOPEDIA OF BIBLICAL ERRANCY

C. Dennis McKinsey – 1995, Prometheus Books, 59 John Glenn Drive, Amherst, New York 14228 – 2197

MALICIOUS INTENT

Sean P. Mactire, Writer's Digest Books –1995, 1507 Dana Ave. Cincinnati, OH. 45207

RELIGION, MAN'S INSULT TO GOD

James McQuity – 1999 Tarpon House Publishing, P.O. Box 771, Tarpon Springs, FL. 34688

THE DEAD SEA SCROLLS, 1947 – 1969

Edmund Wilson, Oxford Press, 1969

A HISTORY OF CHRISTIANITY

Kenneth Scott Latourette, Harper & Row, New York. (Over 1000 pages of sheer drivel, written with laborious love by one thoroughly saturated with Christian bogeyism.)

HEBREW MYTHS: THE BOOK OF GENESIS

Robert Graves & Raphael Patai. Crown Publishers, Inc. N.Y.

THE PASSOVER PLOT

Dr. Hugh J. Schonfield. Distributed by Random House.

Unfortunately, whether by plot or other reasons, many of the authoritative books concerning the real history of the centuries of Catholic Inquisition are no longer available anywhere I have searched. Instead, straight from The Vatican, down throughout its Priesthood, that insufferable period has for years now, been lied about and is now believed, even by sincerely devoted Catholic Priests, to have been a "Spanish Inquisition" carried on by an excommunicated splinter sect. No greater lie has been fabricated since Saul of Tarsus invented Christ.

Printed in the United States
5004

9 781401 049577